The Response to Intervention Documentation Handbook

The Response to Intervention Documentation Handbook

Assessment, Instruction, Intervention

ANDREA OGONOSKY

Park Place Publications, L.P.
Austin, Texas

© 2011 Park Place Publications, L.P.
All Rights Reserved

No part of this book may be reproduced without the
express consent of Park Place Publications, L.P.

512 W Martin Luther King Jr Blvd, #300
Austin, TX 78701
www.ed311.com

First Printing: August 2011
Second Printing: May 2016

ISBN 978-0-9825600-9-9

Certain life experiences define the person we become. My father and brother are two men who demonstrated profound integrity, a strong work ethic, and a loving commitment to family. They positively influenced me to be the best person I can be to my family and to my profession, and I am extremely thankful for having had them in my life, however brief that time may have been.

In loving memory of my father, Andrew Butchko Sr.—
Dad, you have been an angel on my shoulder, guiding me through life for the past forty years. You are always with me.

and

In loving memory of my youngest brother, David—
You are never far from my thoughts and have been deeply missed these past five years.

Contents

Illustrations

Figures

Tables

Forms, Checklists, and Strategies

RtI Fidelity Checklists

Forms designed for team documentation of Tier 1 fidelity, to be
completed every 6 weeks.

RtI Team End-of-Year Review: Tier Summary Data

A concise summary of the campus RtI team's problem solving and
the movement of students across tiers for the school year.

RtI Documentation of Tier 1 Instructional Interventions

Tools for the team to use in recording Tier 1 instructional strategies
and interventions designed to meet evidence-based standards in specific
content areas for identified at-risk students.

Foreword

After several decades of federal involvement in special education, the U.S. Congress did not like what it saw. As of 2004, Congress saw that many students in special education programs did not seem to belong there. Although these students may have been underachieving, their struggles in school did not appear to be based on disability. Rather, the problem was more fundamental—they had not been taught properly.

This observation was coupled with considerable educational research focusing on techniques for instruction in basic skills, especially reading. The conclusion was that our schools need to do a better job of providing instruction in reading and mathematics. The theory was that if schools did a better job of teaching kids to read and to develop math skills, we would see improvements in academic achievement and fewer students identified as having a disability.

What came out of this was Response to Intervention (RtI). RtI theory is simple. If schools will train highly qualified teachers to use scientifically proven methods to teach, and then monitor the results on an individualized basis, we will be able to match every deficit with an appropriate intervention. Kids will do better. Our resources will be used more effectively.

It's a great theory, and one that extends beyond math and reading to other essentials for academic achievement, such as behavior. But it completely depends on the proper use of data. RtI programs demand that decisions about students be based on data rather than teacher intuition or subjective judgments We all know that classroom teachers are already overwhelmed with paperwork. Moreover, data are of no use unless we know how to interpret them properly. How do we create a system of data collection and interpretation that will work in the real world of public school?

This book, by my friend and colleague, Andrea Ogonosky, provides a system that will work. *The Response to Intervention Documentation Handbook: Assessment, Instruction, Interventions* is designed for practical use. Based on her research and many years of experience, Dr. Ogonosky has put together a set of templates that address the key components of a successful RtI program. Those components are built right into the subtitle of the book: assessment, instruction, and interventions. This book brings theory right into the classroom. If properly used by all elements of the school staff, this documentation handbook is sure to lead to better decision making, more consistent instruction, and intelligent interpretation of data. At Park Place Publications, we are very proud to publish *The Response to Intervention Documentation Handbook*.

Jim Walsh
President of Park Place Publications

Acknowledgments

There are many people you rely on to provide support as you go through the process of writing a book. The staff at Part Place Publications are top-notch—thank you for the support and understanding when I sometimes lagged behind because I had a little too much on my plate. Rosemary Wetherold, your excellent editing skills are much appreciated; I learn so much from you. A special thanks to Lexia Learning, particularly Joel Brown and Liz Crawford, to David Stevens from Symphony Math, and to Stewart Pisecco and Roland Espericueta from Psychological Software Solutions for providing sample assessment documentation that wonderfully illustrated examples of strong data sets. For my colleagues at Texas Education Solutions and Spectrum K12, thank you for your continued belief in my work as well as the RtI process. You are indeed special not only to me but also to the many children who benefit from your continued work. Jim Walsh, I am honored for your endorsement of the book. I highly respect your outstanding legal reputation, and I am grateful for our friendship. Thanks to my extended family for their continued support. I am certainly looking forward to sisters' weekend this year! A special thank-you to my beautiful daughters, Kim and Emily, and my husband, James, who continue to support me with their love, kind words, and patience as I dedicated many hours to the completion of this book. I am very blessed!

Introduction

This book is a template for using the correct documentation procedures to deliver effective, high-quality instruction and intervention to at-risk learners within the Response to Intervention (RtI) model. RtI is a system of supports designed to enhance the effectiveness of grade-level curriculum and instruction. It is not intended to be a process for proving, through documentation, that a student needs to be referred for special education testing and programming. If the sole focus of data collection is for referral of students for special education assessment, problems arise because the fidelity of instruction and curriculum, which is essential to a successful RtI program, may be overlooked, and important interventions may be missed.

RtI integrates assessment and intervention in increasing levels of intensity, depending on students' needs. The information gathered is used to maximize student performance academically and behaviorally. Often, problem-solving teams focus their time and energy poorly by focusing on the wrong kind of documentation or collecting information that is not relevant, instead of designing and implementing strong plans. In the spirit of assuring a top-notch RtI system, this book can be used as a guide for documenting the necessary information that will accurately align with appropriate data collection. To aid district- and campus-level documentation of the RtI process, examples of a variety of simplified forms are presented throughout the book.

Strong documentation is required for meeting the legal obligations in supporting students as set forth in the No Child Left Behind Act (NCLB 2001) and the Individuals with Disability Education Improvement Act (IDEA 2004). Chapter 1 considers RtI within a legal context, specifically with reference to the NCLB and IDEA. The chapter also covers the multi-tier RtI model of assessment and instructional decision making as it relates to promoting student achievement. Additionally, this chapter describes each tier, as well as the importance of intensifying data collection in conjunction with intensifying instructional interventions, which, at the end of the RtI continuum, link to referrals for determining eligibility for services under Section 504 of the Rehabilitation Act (1973) or IDEA.

The first step in undertaking assessment is to understand its parameters within an RtI model. Chapter 2 details the multiple sources of data to be collected and documented in order to ensure sound problem solving within the RtI model. Assessment types, differentiated instruction, and problem solving are also discussed in this chapter.

Chapter 3 focuses on correct documentation of access to instruction. It is designed to aid the reader's understanding of how to link curriculum and instructional delivery with RtI campus team's problem-solving strategies.

Chapter 4 explores the "how" of accurately and efficiently documenting assessment that is sufficient for instructional and legal purposes. Ultimately, it is extremely important to promote ease of the assessment collection in order to maintain the integrity of the RtI framework. Assessment must meet standards of reliability and validity, particularly when it is designed to determine access to instruction. Classroom teachers routinely assess students on a regular basis; however, it is imperative that the assessment is connected to clinical utility (it is of practical use).

Assessment provides valuable information regarding trends in student populations and within individual learners, particularly with respect to adequate yearly progress and students' responses to intervention. Equally important is the documentation of students' access to instruction via a thorough review of teacher lesson plans, instructional grouping, and classroom observations focusing on the classroom environment and learners. Chapter 5 presents an in-depth analysis of documenting the use of sound instructional delivery practices linked to student needs within the general education environment (Tier 1 of the three-tier RtI model), as well as within Tiers 2 and 3 (intensified intervention and assessment).

"Fidelity" has become an everyday word in reference of the RtI process and is frequently misunderstood by faculty and other staff. Often, staff perceptions are negative regarding the requirement of fidelity in RtI. Chapter 6 clarifies the importance of fidelity and its documentation and debunks the myths surrounding this type of data collection.

The epilogue contains a handy list of tips for documentation, and in the appendices you'll find a sample district guidance document for RtI, recommended learning style inventories, and a summary of the responsibilities of the case facilitator during Tier 1 consultation. Blank versions of useful forms and checklists for documentation appear in appendix D. The accompanying CD contains both blank and sample completed versions of forms and checklists, as well as the Sample RtI School District Guidance Document contained in appendix A, which can be used as a template.

The Response to Intervention Documentation Handbook

Chapter 1

Why Document?

Legal Context

Response to Intervention (RtI) has been described by the National Center on Response to Intervention (2010) as a multilevel instructional system that integrates assessment and intervention to maximize student achievement and reduce behavioral problems. The core of this instructional process is data-based problem solving, and multiple sources of data are used to design the instructional supports—for the school, the classroom, and the individual student—that promote student achievement. The data collected during the RtI process are used to identify at-risk learners, monitor student progress, provide evidence-based instruction and interventions, adjust the intensity and nature of interventions based on the students' responsiveness to the interventions, and identify students who have learning or other disabilities. Response to Intervention should not be confused as a system that focuses solely on individual students. It also encompasses problem solving to increase the capacity of staff and school systems to achieve adequate yearly progress for all students. The data collected throughout this process should be utilized within a seamless system of supports for students and in essence should be considered part of the reformation of past educational practices.

Educational reform is embedded in legislation that has shaped the foundations of Response to Intervention, beginning with the No Child Left Behind Act of 2001 (NCLB). That act affirms the following two strategies, among others: "holding schools, local education agencies, and States accountable for improving the academic achievement of all students" and "promoting schoolwide reform and ensuring the access of [all] children to effective, scientifically based instructional strategies" [PL 107-110 §1001(4) and (9); emphasis added].

Subsequently, the concept of RtI became rooted in several provisions of federal regulations for the application of "Section 504" and the Individuals with Disability Education Improvement Act (IDEA 2004). What is Section 504? It is a federal civil rights law that is a part of the Rehabilitation Act of 1973. This law ensures protection against discrimination for individuals with disabilities. School-age students fall under the protection of Section 504, which prohibits disability-based discrimination in all school programs and activities in both public and private schools that receive direct or indirect federal funding. The Section 504 definition of the term "disability" and of disability eligibility criteria is different from the IDEA definition. Consequently, many children who are not eligible for protection from discrimination under IDEA are eligible when Section 504 standards are applied. According to the Office for Civil Rights (2011):

> The Section 504 regulations require a school district to provide a "free appropriate public education" (FAPE) to each qualified student with a disability who is in the school district's jurisdiction, regardless of the nature or severity of the person's disability. Under Section 504, FAPE consists of the provision of regular or special education and related aids and services designed to meet the student's individual educational needs as adequately as the needs of nondisabled students are met.

In order to fulfill requirements under Section 504, a school district must recognize its duty to avoid discrimination in policies and practices regarding its personnel and students. School districts have obligations under the law, specifically a responsibility to identify and evaluate students suspected of having a disability. Additionally, the school district must use data to determine whether the disability creates a substantial limitation to the major life activities associated with learning. The determination of a substantial limitation is completed on a case-by-case basis with respect to each student. The Section 504 regulatory provision at 34 CFR 104.35(c) requires that this decision be made by a group of knowledgeable persons and be based on multiple sources of data. Data collection by the campus RtI team in Tier 1 of the RtI model is where the documentation of these decisions begins. (RtI teams are discussed in the next section of this chapter, and details on the tiered model of RtI are presented in the section "RtI Framework" below.)

The greatest misunderstanding of the Response to Intervention process stems from the misperception that RtI team meetings and the activity goals of instructional planning are used primarily to refer students for evaluation and subsequent identification of a learning disability. Although the data gathered by an RtI team are important for decision making, most states require that additional norm-referenced data are also included in eligibility considerations. Simply stated, within the context of IDEA, The purpose of collecting and analyzing RtI data is "to improve the academic achievement and functional performance of children with disabilities, including the use of scientifically based instructional practices, to the maximum extent possible" [20 USC 1400(c)(5)(E)].

To fully understand the complexity of and expectations for establishing a learning disability condition, one must review the statutes and provisions within IDEA, particularly 34 CFR 300.307–311:

1. "[W]hen determining whether a child has a specific learning disability . . . , a local educational agency shall not be required to take into consideration

whether a child has a severe discrepancy between achievement and intellectual ability . . ." [PL 108-446, §614(b)(6)(A)].

2. "In determining whether a child has a specific learning disability, a local educational agency may use a process that determines if the child responds to scientific, research-based intervention as a part of the evaluation procedures . . ." [PL 108-446, §614(b)(6)(B); emphasis added].

3. A local education agency may use up to 15 percent of its federal funding "to develop and implement coordinated, early intervening services . . . for students in kindergarten through grade 12 (with a particular emphasis on students in kindergarten through grade 3) who have not been identified as needing special education or related services but who need additional academic and behavioral support to succeed in a general education environment" [PL 108-446, §613(f)(1)].

In fact, according to Bradley, Danielson, and Hallahan (2002), three primary criteria are associated with eligibility decisions for special education services under the "learning disabled" categorization: the response to research- based interventions is insufficient, low achievement is demonstrated and documented, and exclusionary factors (i.e., intellectual disability, sensory deficits, limited English proficiency [LEP], lack of educational opportunity, and emotional disturbance) are considered.

It is important to review and document the campus RtI team's evaluation of instructional effectiveness in terms of implementation and response. This can be done by simply reviewing and comparing student products and test results with teacher lesson plans to ensure that appropriate instruction was given. Also, the monitoring of student progress is ingrained in many state regulations, and data regarding learning growth (the rate of improvement) must be collected. Although there is little agreement as to defining patterns of inadequate student response, the recommended course of action is to tie a student's goals and expected growth rate patterns to published norms. A determination of low achievement must derive from various aggregated data sources, and care must be taken not to use single-source data. Benchmark, outcome, formative, summative, and normative assessments should align to tell a consistent story regarding the student's individual pattern of learning. Ruling out disorders other than a learning disability is equally important when low achievement has been detected, and if a student's behavior is a factor, one would refer to norm-referenced behavior rating scales for guidance. Finally, the disability decision, which is made by an individualized education program (IEP) committee, must consider the need for specially designed instruction in order for the student to evidence learning growth.

In addition to their impact on individual students, these legal provisions encourage changes in the nature and scope of educational practices in district processes, campus systems, and delivery of curriculum in an effort to promote access to grade-level instruction for all students. Again, as in NCLB and IDEA 2004, there is an emphasis on using student achievement data to foster adequate yearly progress by adjusting the pace and delivery of curriculum and instruction. These data are also used to tie campus accountability (regarding learning) to school improvement plans. Additional emphases in NCLB, IDEA 2004, and, most recently, the American Recovery and Reinvestment Act (ARRA), which President Barack Obama signed in 2009, include promoting and supporting highly qualified teachers, using research-based instruction and interventions, and ensuring safe schools through the use of school- and classroom-based behavior management aligned with positive behavior support. Furthermore, multiple sources of data are necessary for making decisions and for monitoring student progress.

ARRA highlights a school-wide approach to data-based decision making. The intent of this act is to have schools build and enhance student data systems that promote student success and school improvement. Elements of such systems include student demographics, attendance records, formative and summative assessments, benchmark data, grades, archived historical records, curriculum and instructional management, and any information that links instructional practices to state standards.

Within the context of special education, the Child Find provision of IDEA 2004 also has a bearing on RtI documentation. Child Find specifies that schools have a duty to identify, locate, and evaluate students who are suspected of having a disability [20 USC 1412(a)(3); 34 CFR 300.111]. IDEA emphasizes early intervention for students who struggle in school and who possibly need special education services. Response to Intervention is an avenue for providing interventions and supports to such students within the general education setting. While there is much agreement about Child Find, there continues to be much confusion regarding how much intervention a student should receive before being referred for a special education evaluation. This confusion has obviously contributed to tension in the school setting and between parents and school staff, but proper documentation can make a positive difference in the situation. To create a meaningful process for assisting struggling learners, as well as to meet the Child Find requirements, it is essential that the district and campuses follow consistent problem-solving guidelines for decision making. The best way to accomplish this is to develop RtI problem-solving guidelines for district and campus RtI teams. These guidelines can also serve as communication to parents, informing them about how the district will proceed with interventions if their child is struggling in school.

Importance of Documentation

Underlying the proper use and documentation of data is the requirement that the data be collected with integrity and consistency. The instructional leader of the campus sets the culture and tone for correct data collection and documentation. In addition to developing strong staff initiatives on data collection and documentation, the campus administrator needs to establish a highly functional RtI problem-solving team. A strong team consists of five to seven members and can be creatively selected according to the unique needs of the campus. It is suggested that, in addition to the administrator, the team should include teachers representing various grade levels and subjects, curriculum and instructional specialists, and someone trained in data collection and interpretation. It is further recommended that campus administrators maintain a file that documents the procedures used to select and train the team. Specific to team selection, administrators may want to consider staff who

- ✔ Have good communication skills and can act as liaisons between staff and the team.
- ✔ Express knowledge of or an interest in data analysis and interpretation.
- ✔ Have the ability to shift the perceptions and culture of campus staff with regard to making instructional decisions about struggling learners.

To document the campus's support of high-quality data analysis and evidence-based practices, it is recommended that administrators maintain files on the steps taken to develop new skills in team members, such as training in data analysis and team problem solving. Typical topics for professional development opportunities include understanding multiple-source data collection and reporting methods, and how to prevent common mistakes in data analysis and interpretation.

Problem Solving

RtI problem solving is completely rooted in data. Data collection should be naturally occurring and ongoing. It should reflect the educational journey of the student, beginning at the initial entry into school (kindergarten) and ending with the ultimate goal of high school graduation. When a student is at risk for not maintaining progress within the grade-level curriculum, data are used to formulate instructional decisions. RtI problem solving links the assessment data to the instruction and to supplemental supports, which are commonly referred to as interventions. RtI is a prevention-oriented framework for providing timely and efficient support to ensure the student's access to grade-level instruction. Usually, four sources of data are used for problem solving: screening, progress monitoring, diagnostics, and outcomes. These types of assessments and their documentation are discussed in chapter 2.

Additionally, districts need to implement an efficient and effective system that effortlessly integrates data from multiple sources so that the data can be straightforwardly reported to and analyzed by the campus RtI teams. It is crucial that the data be easily available and interpretable; otherwise it will not be used.

RtI Framework

To understand Response to Intervention as a framework for appropriate documentation, it is helpful to remember what RtI is and what it is not. RtI is all of the following:

- An educational effort implemented within the general education system and coordinated with all other services, such as special education, Title I, English language learning (ELL), the Migrant Education Program (MEP), and so on
- A system to provide instructional intervention immediately upon receiving evidence of student need
- A process that determines whether a student responds to scientific, research-based intervention as a part of evaluation procedures
- An alternative approach to the diagnosis of a specific learning disability (SLD). Instead of using the well-known discrepancy model, local education agencies may now use RtI to help establish patterns of a student's strengths and weaknesses.

RtI is not intended to be

- Used solely as a prereferral system. The emphasis should be on prevention first, then layered intervention.
- Implemented by an individual teacher or interventionist.
- Carried out in a separate classroom.
- Implemented as a special education program.
- Put into practice as a separate, stand-alone initiative or system.

Rather, the focus of RtI is on multiple layers of increasingly intensified academic and behavioral supports, most commonly presented as a three-tier model. (See figures 1.1–1.3 for sample three-tier models for secondary schools.)

A simple format for describing RtI to staff and parents is best represented in a district guidance document for RtI (appendix A). This document can present valuable information to staff and parents in a way that also assists the RtI team in maintaining consistent, valid, and reliable documentation of a student's educational history.

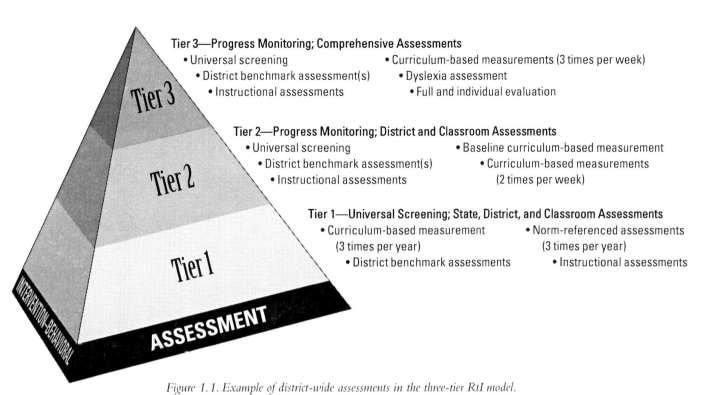

Tier 3—Progress Monitoring; Comprehensive Assessments
- Universal screening
- District benchmark assessment(s)
- Instructional assessments
- Curriculum-based measurements (3 times per week)
- Dyslexia assessment
- Full and individual evaluation

Tier 2—Progress Monitoring; District and Classroom Assessments
- Universal screening
- District benchmark assessment(s)
- Instructional assessments
- Baseline curriculum-based measurement
- Curriculum-based measurements (2 times per week)

Tier 1—Universal Screening; State, District, and Classroom Assessments
- Curriculum-based measurement (3 times per year)
- District benchmark assessments
- Norm-referenced assessments (3 times per year)
- Instructional assessments

Figure 1.1. Example of district-wide assessments in the three-tier RtI model.

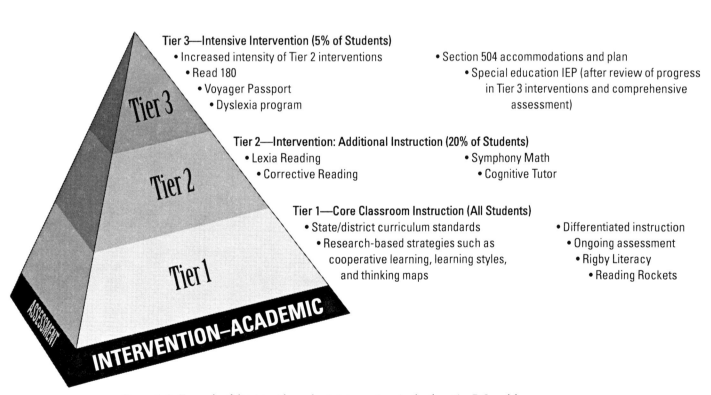

Tier 3—Intensive Intervention (5% of Students)
- Increased intensity of Tier 2 interventions
- Read 180
- Voyager Passport
- Dyslexia program
- Section 504 accommodations and plan
- Special education IEP (after review of progress in Tier 3 interventions and comprehensive assessment)

Tier 2—Intervention: Additional Instruction (20% of Students)
- Lexia Reading
- Corrective Reading
- Symphony Math
- Cognitive Tutor

Tier 1—Core Classroom Instruction (All Students)
- State/district curriculum standards
- Research-based strategies such as cooperative learning, learning styles, and thinking maps
- Differentiated instruction
- Ongoing assessment
- Rigby Literacy
- Reading Rockets

Figure 1.2. Example of district-wide academic interventions in the three-tier RtI model.

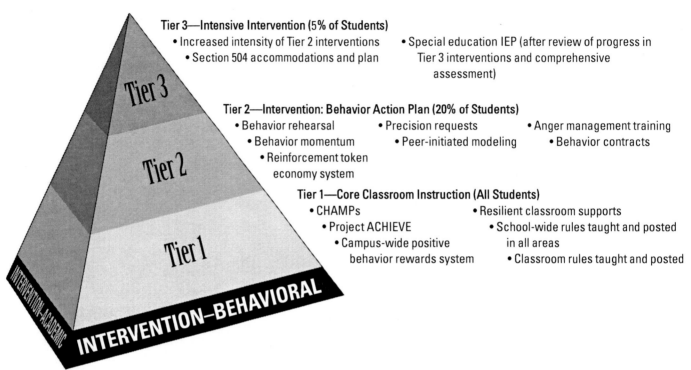

Figure 1.3. Example of district-wide behavioral interventions in the three-tier RtI model.

For further clarification, RtI can be summarized as follows:

Tier 1: Core Instruction and Universal Interventions

Academic	Behavioral
High-quality instruction and learning strategies Differentiated instruction Embedded interventions	School-wide positive behavioral interventions and supports (PBIS) Strong classroom management and clearly articulated expectations Social skills instruction with daily opportunities for rehearsal Proactive discipline policies aligned with PBIS

Tier 1 supporting documentation
✔ Universal screening
✔ Common assessments
✔ Benchmark data

✔ Classroom formative assessments

✔ Classroom summative assessments

✔ Criterion- and norm-referenced assessments

✔ Diagnostic data

✔ Teacher lesson plans

✔ Student products

✔ Classroom fidelity check

✔ Classroom observations (instruction, curriculum, environment, student)

✔ Behavioral multiple-gate data collection (discipline referrals, behavioral screening, parent and teacher interviews)

Tier 2: Supplemental and Targeted Instruction

Academic	Behavioral
Strategic instructional level of student, focused on critical skill development (need-to-knows) Standard protocol (evidence-based and meets NCLB standards) Small-group student-to-interventionist ratio of 5:1	Strategic instruction focused on building age-appropriate interpersonal skills Evidence-based practices aligned with SEL (social, emotional learning) techniques Targeted social skills instruction Peer and adult mentoring and modeling of strategies for social and emotional growth

Tier 2 supporting documentation

✔ Continued Tier 1 documentation

plus

✔ District/campus rubric for decision making: decision rules, aimlines/goals, guidelines for increasing/decreasing support or changing intervention

✔ Focused, continuous progress monitoring and behavior charting (antecedent-behavior-consequence [ABC], frequency, duration, latency) that increases in conjunction with increasing intensity of instruction and intervention

Tier 3: Supplemental and Intensive Instruction

Academic	Behavioral
Increase in strategic, supplemental, and targeted supports Decrease in student-to-teacher ratio to 3:1	Small-group counseling Strategic behavior change plan (behavior action plan) Frequent mentoring Intensified strategies to improve academic engagement time (AET)

Tier 3 supporting documentation
- ✔ Continued Tier 1 documentation
  plus
- ✔ Increased documentation of progress monitoring and behavior charting data
- ✔ Referral for Section 504 or special education evaluation if a pattern of inadequate responses to intervention is detected

• • •

Although there is no single agreed-upon model for Response to Intervention (for example, some models designate special education as its own fourth tier), a common expectation is that an increasing level of intensity of instruction and interventions is necessary to promote student progress. Along with this increasing intensity of instruction there should be a correlational increase in the intensity of documented data collection as well.

Chapter 2

What Is Documented?

Multiple Sources of Data

One of the fundamental benefits of well-done documentation is that it functions as a road map through the information it contains. Proper documentation leads the reader of an RtI plan to the clear conclusion that the instructional and intervention problem solving was based on multiple sources of data (as required by IDEA 2004) and that all aspects of the problem-solving process meet the criteria for fidelity. (Briefly, fidelity is the integrity of the instruction, interventions, and data collection.) Documentation must describe all of the variables that led to the ultimate solution to the problem. Several sources of data flow into the set of documentation that needs to be amassed, including student access to curriculum, delivery of instruction, learning environment (school-wide and classroom), student information, alignment of data with team problem solving, student outcomes (response to interventions), fidelity of the process, and self-evaluation of team problem solving.

Highly Qualified Teachers

Response to Intervention is designed to assist in building and supporting practices that meet the NCLB expectation that all children receive their instruction from highly qualified teachers. According to the US Department of Education (2004), highly qualified teachers must have a bachelor's degree and full state certification or licensure and must prove that they know each subject they teach. Furthermore, states are required to measure the extent to which all students, particularly minority and disadvantaged students, have highly qualified teachers; to adopt goals and plans that ensure that all teachers are highly qualified; and to publicly report on those plans and on the progress made in meeting teacher-quality goals. Additionally, teachers in middle and high schools must have a major in the subject they teach or have course credits equivalent to a major in the subject; must pass a state-developed test; and must meet state-developed criteria (high, objective, uniform state standard of evaluation, or HOUSSE) that demonstrate their subject matter competency, such as providing proof of teaching experience, professional development, and knowledge in the subject garnered over time in the profession. Teachers may also demonstrate their competency by possessing an advanced certification from the state or a graduate degree.

Teacher skills that have been shown to be necessary for student success include the following (Education Commission of the States, n.d.):

✔ Provision of large- and small-group, research-based, differentiated instruction aligned with individual students' developmental levels and learning needs
✔ Understanding of brain-based learning theory and techniques to ensure that adequate learning challenge is achieved
✔ Strong classroom management skills
✔ Use of environmental engineering to promote high academic engagement time
✔ Use of behavioral techniques for effective, positive behavioral interventions and supports

Access to Curriculum

Documentation of a student's access to instruction is critical when an RtI team problem-solves around the student's deficit areas. The first type of information to be documented involves the quality and integrity of the grade-level curriculum and the delivery of instruction. The RtI problem-solving team analyzes and documents the district's core curriculum strands for expected grade-level outcomes. Within the RtI rubric for success (NASDE 2005), a successful Tier 1 is achieved when approximately 80 percent of the students are attaining expected grade-level outcomes without additional instructional or behavioral supports. If more than 20 percent of students are unsuccessful in the core curriculum, then the team assumes that the current core curriculum and instructional practices are not effective. This assumption steers further intervention planning into a systems approach instead of a within-student approach. Instructional and curricular variables should be analyzed to determine where the core curriculum and instruction need to be strengthened.

NCLB (2001) focuses attention on the general curriculum by requiring that states develop "challenging" academic standards for both content and student achievement for all children in at least mathematics, reading/language arts, and, since the beginning of the 2005–2006 school year, science [20 USC 6311(b)(1) (A)–(C)]. The obligation to develop challenging content standards should help states define their general curriculum, and the requirement for states to adopt challenging achievement standards has the potential to raise the quality of the general curriculum. The development of standards is thus a point of intersection for the two major educational statutes: IDEA requires that students with disabilities have access to the general curriculum, according to their individualized needs, while

NCLB helps define and enhance the general curriculum. NCLB also refers, in a number of places, to the use of a high-quality curriculum, further emphasizing what is expected of a state's general curriculum. For example, NCLB discusses the shared responsibility of schools and parents to develop a school-parent compact that describes "the school's responsibility to provide high-quality curriculum and instruction . . . that enables the children served under this part to meet the State's student academic achievement standards" [20 USC 6318(d)(1), emphasis added; see also 20 USC 6311(b)(8)(D) and 6312(c)(1)(O)]. Thus, by requiring that states develop "challenging" content and achievement standards and establish a "high-quality" curriculum, NCLB aims to improve the general curriculum.

Notably, this application of the use of challenging academic standards to all students includes students with disabilities:

> Too often in the past, schools and LEAs [local educational agencies] have not expected students with disabilities to meet the same grade-level standards as other students. The NCLB Act sought to correct this problem by requiring each State to develop grade-level academic content and achievement standards that it expects all students—including students with disabilities—to meet. (67 FR 71710, 71741)

Thus, IDEA and NCLB are aligned with respect to their expectations for the educational performance of students with disabilities: by requiring that students with disabilities have access to the same curriculum according to their individualized needs, IDEA expects that students with disabilities will have the opportunity to meet the educational standards that apply to all children; and NCLB creates the criterion that students with disabilities meet the same standards as students without disabilities.

Instruction

Differentiated instruction is a vigorous way to increase student learning and maximize automaticity of skills. When teachers differentiate instruction through the use of flexible grouping, different instructional materials, or alternate methods of presenting the same content, they promote the progress of all students by attending to vital differences among them (Tomlinson and McTighe 2006). In this era of intense change in our society resulting from the widespread adoption of new technologies (e.g., texting, digital tablets), the need for changing the way instruction is delivered to our students is obvious. As the emphasis in future educational practices shifts to the delivery of instruction, a corresponding shift in perspectives will be needed as well. This shift in perspectives can be maximized through supports the RTI campus team provides, such as teacher consultation and the resources needed for student success. One big change is for teachers to move away from structured lesson plan-

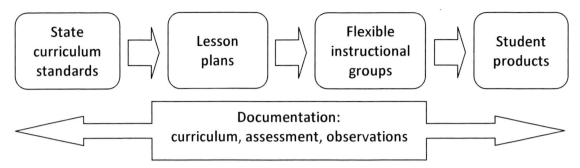

Figure 2.1. Instructional planning.

ning to flexible lesson planning. The model of "one lesson fits all" does not align with differentiated instruction for all. Thus teacher lesson planning must provide opportunities for presenting differentiated instruction. Also, designing classroom instruction that aligns with student learning styles promotes active learning and is important in meeting the diverse needs of learners.

In addition to a shift in instructional delivery, classrooms must be designed to maximize academic engagement time. Therefore teachers must strategically arrange the classroom for increased opportunities for student success. A classroom organized to facilitate differentiated instruction will provide a variety of learning opportunities that engage students at their optimal level of challenge. Many teachers accomplish this by delivering a whole-group lesson and then working with individual students or a small group of students who have similar learning needs while other students work independently, in pairs, or in small groups at student centers. This technique can be documented easily by aligning these activities with student data and using student products as the documentation (see chapter 3 for more on this subject). Ideally the documentation will show a seamless connection between the curriculum, the instruction, and the learner (figure 2.1).

Environment

The importance of the learning environment to student engagement cannot be emphasized too strongly. "Environment" in this context is related to the classroom's structure and events and to behaviors that contribute to or inhibit student learning. The environment is an element of the support system for promoting student interaction with the curriculum and the instruction. The essence of an effective learning environment lies in the teacher's ability to create an atmosphere that is conducive to all learners. Although no one has control over all of the variables in a learning situation, teachers can affect the physical and social context of the instruction. For documenting the environment within an RtI context, the best sources of information are those promoting classroom structure that ensures motivational readiness. Also important for consideration by the RtI team are a classroom climate and culture that build student-teacher relationships and provide a positive and safe setting that reinforces learning.

Assessment

An information collection and management system allows data from continuous progress monitoring to be used to drive instructional decisions throughout the tiered RtI process. Progress-monitoring data indicate student responses to interventions and are used to determine students' movement through the tiers. Academic progress is monitored with increasing frequency as students receive additional, more intensive tiered interventions. Similarly, the RtI team may find it necessary to consider information from assessments of students' attention skills, participation behaviors, communication skills, memory, and social relations with groups, peers, and adults throughout the multi-tier system.

Four types of assessments are used in RtI problem solving: screening, diagnostics, progress monitoring, and outcomes (fig. 2.2). These assessment types are addressed in detail in chapter 4.

Student Information

Collecting student information is an ongoing data documentation process. The historical data to be reviewed for a student include attendance patterns, all assessments, teacher notes on progress, parent-teacher conference information, discipline referrals, previous interventions and their outcomes, and any information parents have supplied (such as outside professional assessments and tutoring results).

Figure 2.2. The four types of assessments used in RtI problem solving.

Data Analysis and Problem Solving

Documentation of the RtI team's problem-solving process is critical. Team problem solving begins with an analysis of the trends of the student population (district, campus, grade, and classroom). This type of analysis should occur three times a year after universal screening has been performed, with the documentation focusing on Tier 1 issues and solutions. The next documentation set tracks the team's process for supporting individual struggling learners who have been identified using multiple sources of data. This documentation follows the RtI model's path for identifying problems (figure 2.3).

The documentation should be clearly written in such a way that each step can be observed and measured. It should include the following elements:

1. A problem identification statement that is based on historical data, universal screenings, classroom observations, student products, and assessment outcomes.

2. An illustration of the systematic collection and interpretation of data related to the student's rate of learning and/or behavioral outcomes over time.

3. An intervention plan that is designed with a layering of intensifying interventions and always includes Tier 1 curricular, instructional, and environmental variables. The plan incorporates baseline data (the starting point of intervention), expected outcome goals, specific evidence-based interventions aligned with student needs, fidelity check expectations and outcomes, and teacher/staff responsibilities.

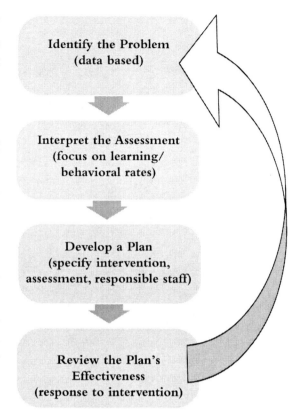

Figure 2.3. The RtI problem-solving process.

4. The RtI team's evaluation of the effectiveness of the plan. This evaluation includes specific data linked to the decision-making rubric designed by the district or campus (e.g., decision rules in progress monitoring such as the three-data-point decision rule, which specifies that after the collection of six data points in progress monitoring, the team evaluates three data points and judges them against the student's goal aimline).

Table 2.1. Data documentation of RtI student support plan

Planning Step	Documentation Action or Decision Needed
Decide on which measures to use.	Reading, mathematics, written expression, content area.
Gather baseline data.	Administer three probes, and use the median score.
Set RtI goal.	Use weekly growth rates based upon local or national standards.
Decide how often to monitor.	1 to 3 times weekly, depending on intensity of intervention (average is 2 times weekly).
Administer curriculum-based measurement (CBM).	Standardized administration, scoring, and charting.
Continue or change intervention-based decision-making rules.	Use trend lines or data-point decision rules.
Document results, and continue problem solving.	Meet at specific time intervals and continue data-based decision making.

The RtI problem-solving documentation should lead those who read it to conclude that data were used to intervene according to the student's needs and were
not used to justify moving the student to another tier in the RtI model and/or
referring the student for a special education evaluation. A student may rise through
the RtI tiers as a result of increasing need; however, it is very important that the
additional student outcome data collected in Tiers 2 and 3 be aligned with the data
supporting Tier 1 access to grade-level instruction. A template may help RtI teams
track their problem-solving progress and organize the related data (see the RtI
Team Documentation Checklist on page 18). Such a form can be attached to the
inside folder of the student's RtI file for easy access and reference.

The intensity of data collection documentation should be closely aligned
with the level of instruction within an RtI framework. For instance, a
Tier 1 curricular support is best documented through naturally occurring Tier 1 instructional data, whereas the documentation for a student
receiving Tier 2 and Tier 3 supports should cover Tier 1 instructional,
plus additional Tier 2 and Tier 3 data.

RtI Team Documentation Checklist

Campus: _____Case Facilitator:_____

Student:_____Grade: ____ Teacher(s): _____

Tier 1 Documentation (ongoing and completed every 6 weeks)
_____ Review of universal screening trends - Dates:_____, _____, _____
_____ Review of lesson plans in area of concern
_____ Review of student work samples
_____ Review of case facilitator consultation documentation
_____ Review of classroom observations focusing on curriculum, instruction, environment, and learner
_____ Review of fidelity checks
_____ Review of 4 sources of assessment (screening, diagnostics, progress monitoring, outcomes)

Note: All sources of documentation are attached to the team meeting form used by the district.

Tier 2 Documentation (weekly progress monitoring and completed every 6 weeks)
_____ Review of intervention design
_____ Review of intervention alignment with diagnostic and progress-monitoring data
_____ Review of student growth (Tier 1 grade level; include all formative assessments and student work samples)
_____ Review of student growth (Tier 2 instructional level, measured by diagnostics and progress monitoring)
_____ Fidelity checks on Tier 2 intervention
_____ Team decisions regarding analysis of multiple sources of data, intervention status, and student support (change in tiers, etc.).

Note: These data are collected with the ongoing Tier 1 data collection.

Tier 3 Documentation (intensified weekly progress monitoring and completed in 4–6 weeks)
_____ Review of intervention design
_____ Review of intervention alignment with diagnostic and progress-monitoring data
_____ Review of student growth (Tier 1 grade level); include all formative assessments and student work samples)
_____ Review of student growth (Tier 3 instructional level measured by diagnostics and progress monitoring)
_____ Fidelity checks on Tier 3 intervention
_____ Team decisions regarding analysis of multiple sources of data, intervention status, and student support (change in tiers, etc.).

Note: These data are collected with the ongoing Tier 1 data collection.

Referral for Section 504 or Special Education Evaluation
_____ Completion of district forms (include all RtI problem-solving information) - Date: _____

Chapter 3

Documenting Curriculum and Instruction

Instructional design and delivery are the hallmarks of connecting a student to grade-level state standards and form the nucleus of a strong RtI process. Because RtI is designed to support struggling learners within the context of general education, sufficient documentation that focuses on student access to appropriate grade-level instruction is essential. Additionally, the IDEA 2004 stipulates that these data must be available for use when determining if a student's underachievement is due to lack of appropriate instruction or to a learning disability.

Access to Instruction

The documentation of access to instruction encompasses information related to the curriculum and to instructional delivery, as well as the RtI team's problem-solving strategies for providing the resources necessary to accomplish access to instruction for all students. Data regarding teacher qualifications and professional development are also included.

Documenting access to instruction in Tier 1 is an important task because at that stage the RtI teams are working to determine whether student underachievement is due to insufficient access to evidence-based instruction, to curriculum issues, or to within-student variables. The heart of Tier 1 documentation is the content, structure, and delivery of instruction. This information is analyzed by examining the elements of lesson plans and their implementation, including differentiated instruction and student grouping, core curriculum support activities, and fidelity of Tier 1 activities. The curriculum is also reviewed for its appropriateness to student population variables. In Tier 1, within-student variables are documented by student work products and assessments. Tier 2 instruction is analyzed by reviewing the student skills that have been targeted for improvement, the alignment of the interventions to those skills, and student assessments. (See chapter 4 for more on assessment.)

Professional Development

Documenting the NCLB requirements for "highly qualified teacher" status is not a job for RtI teams. That task is done by the district's human resources department when a teacher is in the hiring process. The RtI team's role in the area of professional development is one of support. Teams are helpful in promoting the "highly qualified" aspects of teaching using evidence-based practices, particularly those known to be beneficial for at-risk learners. RtI teams assume responsibility for developing proficiency in teachers when a review of campus data (universal screening, district benchmarks, high-stakes tests) indicates that too few students are achieving minimal progress expectations for grade-level success. Remember that, as a general rule, approximately 80 percent of students will meet minimum expectations when Tier 1 instruction is effective.

An RtI team's analysis results in a determination of any insufficiency related to access to instruction. The RtI meeting notes serve as the documentation of any trends the team discovers in the data, as well as any recommendations the team decides to make, such as curricular modifications, additional staff resources, and professional development to address the problem(s).

The team should base its selection of professional development activities on the current skill and knowledge level of the campus staff. In addition, the plan the team chooses must meet NCLB standards. NCLB (2001) describes the term "professional development" as follows:

(A) ["Professional development"] includes activities that
   (i) improve and increase teachers' knowledge of the academic subjects the teachers teach, and enable teachers to become highly qualified;
   (ii) are an integral part of broad schoolwide and districtwide educational improvement plans;
   (iii) give teachers, principals, and administrators the knowledge and skills to provide students with the opportunity to meet challenging State academic content standards and student academic achievement standards;
   (iv) improve classroom management skills;
   (v)(I) are high quality, sustained, intensive, and classroom-focused in order to have a positive and lasting impact on classroom instruction and the teacher's performance in the classroom;
   (II) are not 1-day or short-term workshops or conferences;
   (vi) support the recruiting, hiring, and training of highly qualified teachers, including teachers who became highly qualified through State and local alternative routes to certification;
   (vii) advance teacher understanding of effective instructional strategies that are—

       (I) based on scientifically based research (except that this subclause shall not apply to activities carried out under part D of title II); and

       (II) strategies for improving student academic achievement or substantially increasing the knowledge and teaching skills of teachers; and

 (viii) are aligned with and directly related to—

       (I) State academic content standards, student achievement standards and assessments; and

       (II) The curricula and programs tied to the standards described in subclause (I) except that this subclause shall not apply to activities described in clauses (ii) and (iii) of section 2123(3)(B);

 (ix) are developed with extensive participation of teachers, principals, parents, and administrators of schools to be served under this Act;

 (x) are designed to give teachers of limited English proficient children, and other teachers and instructional staff, the knowledge and skills to provide instruction and appropriate language and academic support services to those children, including the appropriate use of curricula and assessments;

 (xi) to the extent appropriate, provide training for teachers and principals in the use of technology so that technology and technology applications are effectively used in the classroom to improve teaching and learning in the curricula and core academic subjects in which the teachers teach;

 (xii) as a whole, are regularly evaluated for their impact on increased teacher effectiveness and improved student academic achievement, with the findings of the evaluations used to improve the quality of professional development;

 (xiii) provide instruction in methods of teaching children with special needs;

 (xiv) include instruction in the use of data and assessments to inform and instruct classroom practice; and

 (xv) include instruction in ways that teachers, principals, pupil services personnel, and school administrators may work more effectively with parents; and

(B) may include activities that—

 (i) involve the forming of partnerships with institutions of higher education to establish school-based teacher training programs that provide prospective teachers and beginning teachers with an opportunity to work under the guidance of experienced teachers and college faculty;

 (ii) create programs to enable paraprofessionals (assisting teachers employed by a local educational agency receiving assistance under part A of title I) to obtain the education necessary for those paraprofessionals to become certified and licensed teachers; and

 (iii) provide follow-up training to teachers who have participated in activities described in subparagraph (A) or another clause of this subparagraph that are designed to ensure that the knowledge and skills learned by the teachers are implemented in the classroom.

Professional development with respect to RtI should initially focus on providing opportunities for training and coaching in understanding the RtI problem-solving process. Professional development is documented in terms of preparing teachers for RtI in the following areas:

- Universal screening
- Diagnostics
- Progress monitoring
- RtI data analysis and decision making
- Aspects of multi-tier assessment and instruction
- Classroom management

See page 23 for a sample form for documenting staff training.

Once the staff have a clear understanding of the fundamentals of Response to Intervention, specific professional development strands should be developed that pertain to Tier 1:

- Use of planning time to analyze curriculum and instruction
- Development of sound lesson plans
- Balanced literacy instruction
- Instructional grouping
- Brain-based learning
- Differentiated instruction
- Positive behavior supports

It is equally important that the building administrator maintain a record of professional development activities in which all campus staff participate. To achieve fidelity of this process, it is recommended that the principal keep attendance sheets and records of the goals of staff development activities. It is also suggested that, when appropriate, the principal obtain a copy of the professional credentials of the persons hired to train staff.

Teacher Collaboration

Scheduled planning time is essential for effective teacher preparation and teaming (Flowers, Mertens, and Mullhall 1999) and is also very important for building strong professional learning communities within schools. Planning time provides the necessary opportunity for teachers to collaboratively resolve curricular problems, create robust lesson plans, and discuss common issues (such as student

RtI Team Documentation: Staff Training

TIER 1 *High-quality instructional and behavioral supports are provided for all students within general education.*

	Training Date	Coaching Date	Teacher Implementation Date
Universal screening	_____	_____	_____
Diagnostics	_____	_____	_____
Progress monitoring	_____	_____	_____

Description of Content
- Collection and sharing of benchmark data among teachers, principals, district staff, and parents (data are collected in fall, winter, and spring)
- Specific, objective measures of problem areas, not anecdotal information or opinions

TIER 2 *Students whose performance and rate of progress lag behind those of peers in their classroom, school, or district receive more-specialized prevention or remediation within general education.*

	Training Date	Coaching Date	Teacher Implementation Date
Baseline data collection	_____	_____	_____
Diagnostics	_____	_____	_____
Progress monitoring	_____	_____	_____
Written plan of accountability	_____	_____	_____
Comparison of pre- and post-intervention data	_____	_____	_____

Description of Content
- Curriculum-based measurement (CBM) to determine whether the problem area is an issue with the student or the core curriculum
- Which interventions will be tried that are different? Who will deliver them? When? Where? For how long?
- Frequent collection of a variety of data for examining student performance over time and evaluating interventions, in order to make data-based decisions
- Data-based decision making for intervention effectiveness

TIER 3 *Tier 3 includes all the elements of Tier 2. The difference between Tier 2 and Tier 3 is the frequency and group size of the intervention treatment.*

	Training Date
Increased intensity of interventions	_____

Description of Content
- The most intensive phase of RtI
- Fidelity of intervention ensured by documentation
- Referral for multidisciplinary assessment for special education if progress monitoring does not establish improvement after intervention phase is implemented

Source: Adapted from Ogonosky, Booth, and Cheramie 2006.

grouping, delivery of instruction, the use of technology, and resources needed for success). Teachers can also use this time to evaluate all aspects of the lesson plans. Documentation regarding curriculum and instruction can occur naturally during teacher collaboration meetings (e.g., using a meeting agenda that describes teacher preparation for delivery of instruction).

To determine the alignment of the curriculum with state standards, most school districts convene a curriculum team composed of teachers, department leaders, content specialists, and administrators. Together, the team members create a curriculum framework that remains a work in progress—it is modified and adapted as necessary over time to ensure the curriculum's compliance with state standards. This framework should be designed to meet the educational needs of all students and should describe the content and skills being taught in all classrooms. The framework's description is written clearly and concisely in a format conducive to use in lesson planning, and the curriculum itself is aligned vertically to facilitate communication among educators. Vertically aligning a curriculum is planning the curriculum across grade levels, starting at kindergarten and continuing through high school. When a district's curriculum is aligned vertically, student performance is strengthened and there is less need for reteaching foundational skills. Because the curriculum is adopted by the district and implemented according to the district's mission or vision, the adopted curriculum framework serves as the curriculum's documentation.

In instances when the appropriateness of a student's interaction with the instruction is a concern, an efficient way to document a Tier 1 evaluation of a lesson plan is to have a team-assigned case facilitator visit with the student's teachers during a common planning time so that they can review the plan together. Using a lesson-plan evaluation rubric to drive the discussion is encouraged. The rubric may be filled out collaboratively by the case facilitator and teachers and then discussed at the next scheduled RtI team meeting. An example of a Tier 1 lesson-plan review rubric is presented on pages 25–26.

In order for planning times to be effective and efficient, an administrator may design the campus schedule to give all teachers at each grade or subject level one common planning time per week. To promote a thorough documentation trail for these planning times, carry out the following suggestions:

- ✔ Verify attendance with a sign-in sheet.
- ✔ Keep a copy of the agenda, and make sure it is dated.
- ✔ Save teacher work products created during the planning time, such as common lesson plans and ideas for independent work activities in the classroom.

RtI Team Documentation: Tier 1 Lesson Plan Review

Teacher: _____   Content Area: _____   Grade: _____   Date of Review: _____

Lesson Plan Element	Excellent (4 points)	Accomplished (3 points)	Satisfactory (2 points)	Beginning (1 point)	Score
Alignment with state standards	Lesson supports core curriculum, aligned to state standards. Benchmarks are stated and appropriately used to guide lesson plan development.	Lesson provides connections to core curriculum, referenced to state standards. Benchmarks are stated and connected to lesson plan development.	Lesson appears to relate to core curriculum and state standards, but alignment is not explicit. Benchmarks are stated but not explicitly connected to lesson plan development.	Lesson does not provide connection to core curriculum or state standards. Benchmark information is absent.	
Instructional goals and objectives	Goals and objectives are stated clearly and aligned to standards incorporating concepts, principles, and cognitive skills within the area of study. Lesson plan provides a list of student outcomes at end of lesson. Learners can determine what they should know and be able to do as a result of instruction.	Goals and objectives are stated. Objectives are listed and reference standards. Learners are able to determine what they should know and be able to do as a result of instruction.	Goals and objectives are provided but are not clear and might not be realistic, given the lesson content. Objectives do not sufficiently address benchmarks.	Objectives are not listed, are unclear, and do not align with state standards or benchmarks.	
Instructional strategies	Differentiated instructional strategies are stated clearly and aligned with evidence-based practices. Lesson procedures are complete, deep, and flexible. Lesson offers extensions for higher-level learning, and adaptations are evident for students with special needs. Plan identifies potential barriers to lesson and offers alternative instructional strategies.	Most strategies are appropriate to learning and are evidence based. Lesson procedures are complete but lack depth in details for adapting lesson for higher-level learning. Plan is not complete in adaptations for students with special needs. Lesson is not clear on addressing potential barrier, nor does it offer alternative strategies.	Some strategies are appropriated and have evidence-based support. Procedure lacks depth and does not offer strategies for adaptations to students with higher-order learning or special needs. Teacher may need to seek out resources for completion of lesson.	Instructional strategies are missing or are not appropriate to lesson content. Lesson appears incomplete. Teacher role is not clearly defined. Teacher will need to invest significant time and effort in order to implement lesson.	
Learning tasks	Tasks are listed that are aligned with goals and objectives of lesson. Task concepts are engaging in reasoning, reflection, analysis, and synthesis of learning and evaluation of information. Students create their own product/process. Tasks build on previously learned information and require student to build on that knowledge. Authentic learning experiences are provided.	Most tasks are aligned with goal and objectives. Most tasks are engaging in reasoning, reflection, analysis and synthesis of learning and evaluation of information. Tasks require students to investigate and create their own product/process. Most tasks build on previously learned information.	Tasks are somewhat aligned to goals and objectives. The tasks engage students in the application of previously learned material using multiple representations, but students are not required to make connections among them.	Tasks listed are tangentially related to goals and objectives. Tasks require only limited practice. Student task completion relies on recall and identification only of previously learned information. The structure of the tasks listed does not encourage intrinsic motivation.	

1 of 2

Lesson Plan Element	Excellent (4 points)	Accomplished (3 points)	Satisfactory (2 points)	Beginning (1 point)	Score
Resources	All needed materials are listed. Necessary supplies are readily accessible through technology or teacher resources center.	Plan has a materials list but is missing some details. Most supplies appear to be available through technology or teacher resource center.	Plan has a materials list, but important details may be missing such as quantity and type of materials. Tangential connections to technology resources are listed.	Items essential for plan implementation are not evident or listed. Details are omitted, and little information is available regarding access to technology or teacher resources.	
Assessment	Assessments are aligned with benchmarks and lesson objectives. Strategies are described in detail for data collection. Rubrics for scoring are included. Design of assessment is for progress monitoring, feedback, and differentiation of content.	Some assessments are aligned with benchmarks and lesson objectives. Design of assessment is diagnostic and evaluative, with some reference to progress monitoring.	Assessments appear related to benchmarks and lesson objectives. Assessment information is vague and may or may not be designed to drive instruction.	There is no evidence of assessment connected to benchmarks or lesson objectives. Reference to assessment relies solely on paper-and-pencil tasks or outcomes.	
Use of technology	Plan provides information for access to real-world situations through video, audio, graphics. Multisensory applications are represented and provide multiple opportunities for skill building. Selection and application of technology are appropriate to learning environment and outcomes.	Plan provides for use of technology to enable students to be meaningfully involved in real-world applications using video, audio, graphics. Lesson's use of technology encourages student involvement in use of technology and is appropriate.	Plan lists technology but is not focused and does not drive student involvement to affect learning outcomes.	Plan lists technology that is not appropriate to learning outcomes or environment. The technology treats students as passive recipients of information and is not clearly designed.	
Total points per column					

Scoring Rubric for RtI Team Documentation of Tier 1 Lesson Plan Review

27–28 points: Excellent   25–26 points: Accomplished   23–24 points: Satisfactory   Below 23 points: Beginning

Note: If score is below 23, team will problem-solve to determine which supports are needed and how the lesson plan needs to be redesigned to align at-risk learners with access to curriculum and instruction.

2 of 2

Environment

With regard to the learning environment, it is important to document that students have been provided with adequate learning time in core subjects. The following are some example items that can serve as documentation in this area:

- A copy of the campus master schedule
- Teacher lesson plans reflecting direct instruction combined with small-group activities
- Student products

The RtI team can also document teacher strategies for increasing academic engagement time, by completing a strategic review of evidence-based indicators. A completed example of a simple form to use in Tier 1 for this type of documentation is on page 28.

Academic engagement time is an important indicator of student success. A student's engagement is affected by the environment surrounding curriculum delivery and the instructional techniques the teacher uses. According to Ogonosky and Mintsioulis (2010), classrooms need to be organized to enhance learning. Documentation of the environment will thus include a description of the overall climate of the classroom. In addition, students tend to prosper in environments where they feel comfortable and can build relationships. A research study by Furrer and Skinner (2003) concluded that enhancing the quality of students' relationships should be a priority for schools. Activities that contribute to a safe and nurturing educational environment and promote the quality of relationships in the classroom should therefore be documented.

The easiest way to document the characteristics of the learning environment is to conduct classroom observations. (See the RtI Classroom Observations form on page 29 as an example.) Classroom observations can be scheduled if the RtI team determines, through data analysis, that academic engagement time needs to be increased or if concern is raised that a specific student needs additional instruction and support. Areas to focus on when observing the classroom environment include these:

- ✔ Physical arrangement of the room (furniture layout, organization of equipment and supplies)
- ✔ Access to technology to increase task engagement
- ✔ Prominent posting of rules
- ✔ Evidence of established learning routines
- ✔ Expectations for work completion (graphic organizers, visual representations of completed work samples)

RtI Team Documentation: Tier 1 Instructional Strategies for Increasing Academic Engagement Time

Teacher/Content Area: _____   Student: ____Carrie Dunn____   Date: ___1/23/11___

Key Points	Salient Features	Consistency of Implementation	Fidelity Check
High-quality, research-based activities	(Yes) No Are aligned with state curriculum standards/content objectives. (Yes) No Are rigorous and relevant to content designed for high student interest and multisensory involvement. (Yes) No Provide students with choice of activity. (Yes) No Assess student age, interests, needs, learning styles, and developmental level when designing activity. Yes (No) Use a variety of activities in order to avoid practice effects and saturation, which can inhibit on-task engagement.	Attendance Work Samples Classroom Observations Notes: All are attached.	Fidelity Check - No Classroom Observations Lesson Plan Review Notes: Fidelity checks will be completed on 2/15/11.
Positive outcomes for students	(Yes) No Students take ownership in their learning. (Yes) (No) Student engagement increases when students are presented with activities based on their interest and ability level. Yes (No) Allowing for choice of product increases student motivation. (Yes) No Ability to build foundational skills increases when activity is individualized for students.	Classroom Observations Notes: Did not observe students having choice in assignments, and assignments were not differentiated. Will work with Mrs. Smith on developing alternate assignments for flexible groups.	Classroom Observations
Teacher planning	(Yes) No Review curriculum strands based on state expectations. (Yes) No Determine which materials and resources are necessary. (Yes) No Align activity with direct instruction embedded in lesson plans. (Yes) No Determine product assessment tool (e.g., rubrics) and evaluation methods. (Yes) No Plan for sharing with grade/content teachers.	Notes: Case facilitator reviewed planning meetings and determined that teachers work collaboratively to develop resources needed for lesson plan content.	Lesson Plan Review

We assure that the above-noted intervention(s) were conducted as disclosed.

_____   _____   _____
Principal/ RtI Team Chair   Classroom Teacher/Service Provider   Case Facilitator

RtI Classroom Observations

Student:_____ Grade:_____ Date of Observation: _____

Teacher: _____ Campus: _____

Observer: _____ Time of Day: From _____ to _____

Teacher-Student Ratio:_____ Instructional Level of Lesson: _____

Time on Task: *(Circle* **on task** *[+] or* **off task** *[−] at 10-second intervals.)*

+ −	+ −	+ −	+ −	+ −	+ −	+ −	+ −	+ −	+ −	+ −	+ −	+ −	+ −	+ −

Class/Subject Observed: *(Observation should be in the area of suspected disability.)*

○ English/LA	○ Reading	○ History/Social Studies	○ Science
○ Math	○ Specials	○ Other:	○ Other:

Student-Teacher Ratio during Observation Period:

Students:	○ Fewer than 10	○ 10–15	○ 16–20	○ More than 20

Classroom Arrangement:

○ Rows of desks	○ Grouped desks	○ Tables	○ Centers	○ Other:

Classroom Interaction with Teacher:	Yes	No	Not Observed	Comments:
Demanded teacher attention	○	○	○	
Was attentive to instruction/instructor	○	○	○	
Had excessive concern with achievement	○	○	○	
Participated in class discussion	○	○	○	
Responded appropriately to: Praise	○	○	○	
Correction	○	○	○	
Required firm discipline	○	○	○	
Was out of seat without permission	○	○	○	

Work Behavior:				
Began tasks promptly	○	○	○	
Had short attention span	○	○	○	
Was easily distracted	○	○	○	
Appeared prepared and organized for activity	○	○	○	
Follows oral instruction	○	○	○	
Follows written instruction	○	○	○	
Works effectively in: Small group	○	○	○	
Large group	○	○	○	
Alone	○	○	○	
Appears to work to limit of ability	○	○	○	

Classroom Interaction with Peers:				
Interacts with peers appropriately	○	○	○	
Disturbed others: Frequently	○	○	○	
Occasionally	○	○	○	
Not at any time	○	○	○	

Comments: _____

_____

_____

Signature of Observer _____ Position _____

✔ Student–teacher interactions during instruction
✔ Peer interactions during independent work activities and small-group lessons
✔ Instructional level of tasks presented
✔ Task demands

•   •   •

In my experience, many questions arise from parents and staff when there is a concern (or dispute) about the level of instruction that a struggling student needs in order to achieve grade-level success. Therefore it is very important that the RtI team use information that has been documented in a natural and organized manner, reflecting everyday data collection and analysis connected with ongoing classroom instruction. The suggestions and strategies described in this chapter are simple and effective solutions for dynamic documentation of students' access to instruction.

Chapter 4

Documenting Assessment

In this era of accountability in schools, there is strong advocacy for increasing the amount of assessment data to be collected and used for instructional planning. One of the fundamental flaws of this current focus on compiling school assessment data is that the data often are not used effectively and efficiently after they are collected. Thus, for many teachers, administrators, parents, and RtI teams, what to *do* with the data remains unclear.

In its purest sense, *assessment is the foundation of all problem solving in the RtI process.* Assessment enables teachers to identify what students are learning, as well to monitor student progress toward meeting grade-level and instructional-level goals. But problems arise when teachers—with very little guidance or supervision—are asked to make sense of vast amounts of existing student assessment results. It is not uncommon for a teacher to administer assessments, score them, and then place a report of the results in the student's educational file. Often, not much else is done with the data unless the student starts to lag far behind.

To obtain real benefits from assessments, it is essential that collected data be used in an organized way. Then teachers will be able to use the results in a consistent manner to gain insight about student progress and take appropriate proactive and preventive actions. Assessment results can also be the basis of discussions among staff on how instruction can be monitored and adjusted to the needs of each learner. The goal of the RtI team is to guide all staff to take this approach with assessment, and the team should document the effective use of the data.

To build consistency into data collection and analysis, the following effective assessment practices are recommended:

✔ Assessment is ongoing and monitors student progress.
✔ Assessment functions as the barometer for measuring the effectiveness of instruction and lesson planning.
✔ Assessment readily detects students who are struggling with certain aspects of the curriculum goals and objectives.
✔ Assessment drives all decision making for curricular accommodations and adaptations.

✔ Assessment data are used to design additional curricular support that builds on student strengths and incorporates evidence-based techniques.

✔ Assessment data are used in developing flexible student grouping in classrooms that is aligned with the students' strengths and needs.

An effective assessment plan has four main objectives:

1. To *identify* students at the beginning of the year who are at risk or experiencing difficulties and may need extra instruction or intensive interventions in order to progress toward grade-level standards by the end of the year, as well as students who have reached benchmarks and need to be challenged. Identification begins with a sound screening instrument.

2. To *monitor* students' progress during the year to determine whether at-risk students are making adequate progress in critical skills and to identify any students who are either falling behind or need to be challenged.

3. To *inform* instructional planning in order to meet the most critical needs of individual students.

4. To *evaluate*_whether the instruction or intervention provided is powerful enough to help each student achieve grade-level standards by the end of each year.

Universal Screening	**Diagnostic Assessment**
• Is a brief assessment of critical skills known to be strong predictors student performance • Is given to all students three times per year • Is reliable and valid • Establishes a grade-level baseline of critical academic and behavioral skills • Identifies campus, grade, and classroom deficits in curriculum and instruction • Identifies students who are at risk of falling behind in grade-level standards • Measures fluency rate (reading, math)	• Is a lengthy assessment that produces an in-depth analysis of targeted skills • Provides information for planning more-effective curriculum and instruction • Is administered in conjunction with a clear plan of intervention • Presents updated information about a student's academic or behavioral skills • Is used to help plan more-powerful instruction or interventions
Outcomes Assessment	**Progress Monitoring**
• Is given at the end of the school year • Is used for school, district, and/or state reporting purposes • Provides school leaders and teachers feedback about the overall effectiveness of their instructional program	• Is a brief, frequent assessment • Determines a student's skill needs • Detects the rate of a student's progress • Provides information on the effectiveness of instruction • Is used at decision points related to a student's movement within or between tiers • Identifies the need for additional assessment

Figure 4.1. The four types of data collected through ongoing RtI assessment.

Table 4.1. Universal screening data for second-grade students: oral reading fluency

Teacher: Mrs. Smith Student Name	Oral reading fluency (WCPM)[a]	Below fall-semester cut score (25 WCPM)?[a]
Akira	30	
Emily	32	
Daniel	27	
Jaquin	27	
Kyesia	*12*	*Deficit/at risk*
Cayden	*23*	*Deficit/at risk*
Jessie	*19*	*Deficit/at risk*
Belita	*18*	*Deficit/at risk*
Mitchell	39	
Katherine	29	
Kimberly	*14*	*Deficit/at risk*
Ben	28	
Kindra	31	
Andy	30	
Jada	*11*	*Deficit/at risk*
Pilar	27	

[a]WCPM, words correct per minute. : J. Hasbrouck and G. A. Tindal. 2006. Oral reading fluency norms: A valuable assessment tool for reading teachers. 59 (7): 636–644.

Four types of data are collected through the ongoing assessment process of RtI, and these must be documented. A summary of the four types of assessments used to collect these data is presented in figure 4.1.

Universal Screening

Universal screening is administered three times per year and focuses on oral reading fluency or comprehension (maze); a mixture of basic facts and concepts and applications for math; and correct writing sequence for writing. Screening may also be conducted for content areas such as academic vocabulary, concepts and understanding of essential skills, literal and inferential comprehension, and skimming and scanning (Ogonosky 2009). According to Batsche et al. (2005), universal screening yields data that are useful for evaluating class performance and identifying resources for teachers. It also aids in the identification of students who need further assessment for increased intensity of instructional intervention (Tier 2). The RtI campus team is responsible for using screening data to support general education classroom teachers in providing sound differentiated teaching strategies to help all learners meet state-mandated core curriculum standards. An example of recorded universal screening data is shown in table 4.1. Sample documentation of Tier 1 problem solving (on page 34) includes an RtI team's analysis of similar data and the team's proposed action plan.

RtI Team Documentation: Tier 1 Problem Solving

(Complete this form after universal screenings have been administered.)

Campus: _____North Elementary_____ Date: _9/20/10_ Date of Screening: _10/4/10_

Grade: __1__   Area: Reading _X_ Math _____   Cut Score: __25 WCPM__

TEAM DATA ANALYSIS

Data Trends: A review of grade 1 reading fluency data showed that 82% of all grade 1 students met minimum expectations on the fall universal screening in reading. Mrs. Smith's class data did not reflect this, however. According to the universal screening results, only 62% of her students met the minimum cut score of 25 WCPM (words correct per minute). A further review of the classroom environment reveals that 4 of the 6 students identified as being at risk are ESL learners with a dominant language of Spanish. The other 2 students have participated in a preschool program for at-risk learners.

PLAN OF ACTION FOR TIER 1 CURRICULUM AND INSTRUCTION

Mrs. Smith will be given support from the campus bilingual specialist in designing lesson plan objectives to meet the needs of the 4 ESL learners in developing English language skills along with their additional ESL support. These 4 students will be monitored by both the classroom teacher and the bilingual specialist, using formative assessments to determine the efficacy of the Tier 1 added instruction.

A case facilitator will be assigned by the RtI team to the 2 other students to begin monitoring their progress on additional differentiated instructional techniques, after Mrs. Smith gives both students a learning style inventory. The case facilitator will then begin documentation of student progress on Tier 1 instruction and support.

MEMBERS IN ATTENDANCE

_____   _____

_____   _____

_____   _____

_____   _____

Another method for recording universal screening data is to create a bar graph based on the data. See figure 4.2 for an example.

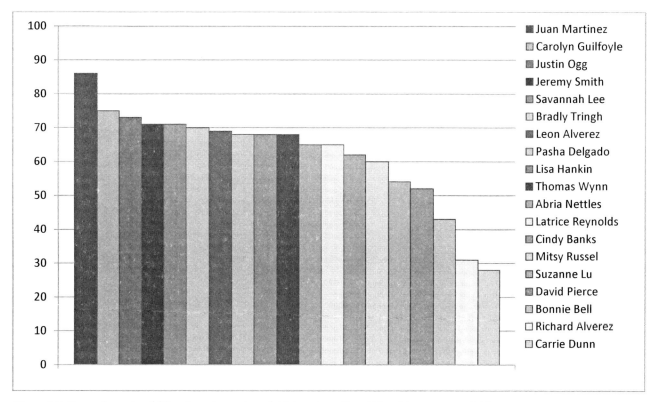

Figure 4.2. Example results of fall universal screening of third-grade reading skills, with a cut score of 44.

Diagnostics

According to McKenna and Dougherty Stahl (2009), diagnostic assessments yield information that is helpful for planning instruction. The scope of the tests may focus on multiple skill sets and be representative of multiple tasks that students are asked to perform. For RtI documentation purposes, the team analyzes diagnostic data and then develops evidence-based instruction and interventions aligned with identified skill deficits. Diagnostic assessments are a way to determine which types of interventions are necessary to support student achievement in either grade-level (Tier 1) or instructional-level (Tier 2 or 3) instruction. It is very important that all staff have a good understanding of the various diagnostic tools available to them and, most importantly, an awareness of how to interpret and use the results of the assessments.

The types of assessments that are considered diagnostic in nature are regularly administered in a consistent manner throughout the school year. These tests may be developed by the district curriculum committee or commercially purchased (as part of an intervention series). They can be paper-and-pencil tests or tests that are given on a computer. The primary kinds of assessments that provide diagnostic in-

Class Table

	Name	Grade	Performance Predictor	Teacher Directed Lexia Lessons	Recommended Software Usage (Avg Mins/Week)	Actual Software Usage (Avg Mins/Week)	Current Assignment (Level of Material)	Certificate Available
				Prescription of Intensity				
	Aviles, Oscar	1st	100%		20-40	53	PR L4 (Beg 2nd)	
!	Diehl, Thoraya	1st	100%	📝	20-40	53	PR L4 (Beg 2nd)	
	Prado, Jessica	1st	100%		20-40	55	PR L4 (Beg 2nd)	
!	Shuler, Priscilla	1st	100%	📝	20-40	57	PR L5 (Mid 1st)	
	Wetzel, Luis	1st	100%		20-40	58	PR L4 (Beg 2nd)	
!	Rockwell, Juan	1st	75%	📝	40-60	49	PR L3 (Mid 1st)	
	Yost, Karla	1st	75%		40-60	23	PR L3 (Mid 1st)	🏆 Last Week
	Donald, Adrian	1st	50%		60-80	38	PR L2 (Beg 1st)	
!	Durant, Jacob	1st	50%	📝	60-80	13	PR L2 (Beg 1st)	
!	Fugate, Kyle	1st	50%	📝	60-80	25	PR L2 (Beg 1st)	
	Gauthier, Anthony	1st	50%		60-80	32	PR L2 (Beg 1st)	
	Kowalski, Vincent	1st	50%		60-80	52	PR L2 (Beg 1st)	
!	Newsom, Alexa	1st	50%	📝	60-80	30	PR L2 (Beg 1st)	
!	Paquette, Kaleigh	1st	50%	📝	60-80	40	PR L2 (Beg 1st)	
	Portillo, Jacob	1st	50%		60-80	14	PR L2 (Beg 1st)	
!	Mize, Ebony	1st	15%	NA	80-100	33	ER L1 (Pre K)	

! Indicates Instruction Needed.   Learn More about Level of Material.

Figure 4.3. Example of software-generated documentation of the use of a prototypical reading intervention program (Lexia Reading) in a teacher's home class.

formation regarding student performance are classroom formative and summative assessments (grade-level), district common assessments, district benchmark assessments, district formative assessments, curriculum-based measurements, and student work samples. Many states also require certain diagnostic testing of students, such as the Differential Reading Assessment (second edition), the TPRI (Texas Primary Reading Inventory), Illinois Certification Testing System (ICTS) Basic Skills test, and so on.

When a student is receiving a Tier 2 intervention, districts often choose to purchase a software program as part of the intervention. Many of the research-based software programs available to support student learning offer diagnostic tools consistent with the student's needs. These diagnostic tools should be used, and the software-generated report of the results should be presented at follow-up RtI meetings. An example of documentation recording the use of a reading intervention program, Lexia Learning, in a teacher's home class is shown in figure 4.3.

Progress Monitoring

Progress monitoring data can be obtained via many different types of assessment, including formative assessments. The most commonly used progress-monitoring assessment that helps determine a student's learning rate is curriculum-based measurement (CBM). CBM is a set of timed techniques, commonly referred to as probes. The probes are simplistic in design, supported by many years of research, and based on common sense (they measure what is being taught). CBM can be cost-efficient because it can be accomplished using readily available curricular materials. There is a standardized method of administration, scoring, and interpretation, and it requires minimal staff training because it is easy to do.

Within the context of RtI, Tier 2 and 3 supports must be matched to the student's instructional level (not grade level). Instructional matching is considered the key to identifying the entry point of the intervention. The campus RtI team must know where in the curriculum the instructional intervention should be introduced, and must also use the appropriate pace of delivery of the intervention. CBM data allow the team to do this by matching the learner with tasks that are appropriately challenging while providing a realistic opportunity for success.

The outcome measure in CBM is fluency rate. This rate forms the basis of the problem-solving team's determination of the student's rate of skill acquisition, which in turn establishes an appropriate rate of delivery of instruction within the intervention phase. Knowing a student's fluency rate also aids the team in identifying the retention rate of the struggling learner. The retention rate reflects the student's ability to retain and meaningfully use information that has been delivered via the instructional intervention. Typically this information is most helpful in analyzing the student's responses to the interventions. Progress-monitoring data are usually documented in a graph format (see figure 4.4 for an example), with the date of administration of the CBM probe on the horizontal axis and the number of correct responses on the vertical axis. With all CBM assessments a baseline data point is obtained. This baseline score indicates the student's instructional level in the curriculum prior to the strategic intervention stage and is used as a point of comparison by the RtI team as it determines the effectiveness of intensified interventions.

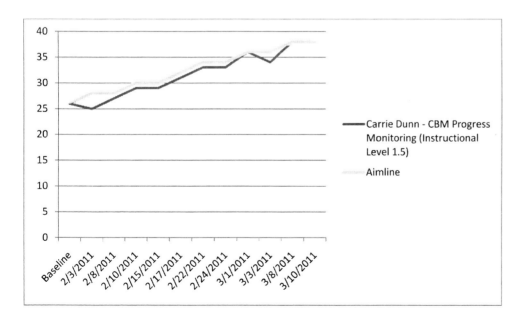

Figure 4.4. Example of CBM progress-monitoring data documented in a graph format, with the date of administration of the CBM probe on the horizontal axis and the number of correct responses on the vertical axis.

Next, the team determines an appropriate instructional growth rate after a pre-determined period of time (known as the outcome goal). Once a student's outcome goal for instruction/intervention is established, the RtI team should begin weekly progress monitoring as the intervention is implemented and plot the CBM data points on a graph. Many districts design and use their own forms for the graphs, but if a commercial prototypical intervention is being used, it may include a diagnostic progress monitor. Examples of prototypical intervention reports from Symphony Math are shown in figures 4.5 and 4.6.

The most challenging aspects of RtI documentation of behavior are collecting data linked to the positive behavior supports implemented in Tier 1 and monitoring individual student progress in Tiers 2 and 3. The handbook *RtI—Three Tiers of Behavior* (Ogonosky and Mintsioulis 2010) provides guidance into designing a process that supports natural documentation of behavioral RtI. However, a lack of understanding remains among many staff members about the necessity of collecting information to document the effectiveness of the behavioral interventions with integrity. Examples provided by Psychological Software Solutions Inc. (figures 4.7–4.9) emphasize the systematic and strategic collection of behavioral data by the campus RtI team when monitoring student progress.

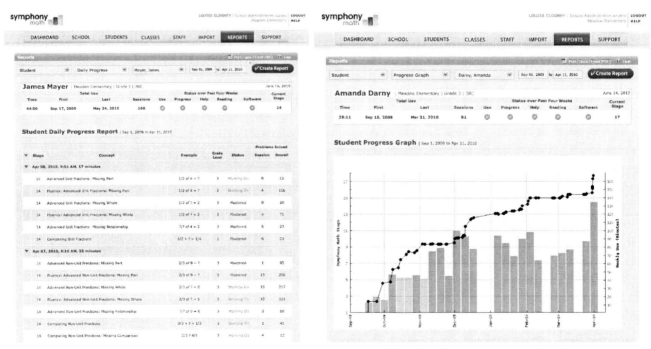

Figure 4.5. Example of natural documentation of an individual student's progress, via a report generated by a prototypical math intervention program (Symphony Math).

Figure 4.6. Example of how one prototypical math progress-monitoring intervention system (Symphony Math) documents student progress over time.

Figure 4.7. Sample progress-monitoring report for an individual student on a single behavioral objective: "Works satisfactorily on activities and completes assignments with 75% accuracy." (Report produced by Review360 software, from Psychological Software Solutions Inc.)

Figure 4.8. Sample documentation of the effectiveness of a positive behavior support strategy (preferential classroom placement), as part of an individual student's behavior intervention plan. (Report produced by Review360 software, from Psychological Software Solutions Inc.)

Summary Report   ✖

From: 08/01/2010   To: 07/15/2011   **Update**

Review360
Behavior Matters

Student Progress Summary Report
Student Support Team Plan
8/1/2010 - 7/15/2011
Report Generated on 7/15/2011

ARELLANO, ALLEN
GRADE: OTHER / NOT SPECIFIED   **STUDENT ID:** 321012099

Lead Teacher: Gentry, Andrew
North Elementary, Review360 District

PLAN STATUS

DAYS OF DATA	DAYS SCORED	DAYS ABSENT
24	24	0

STRATEGIES

	RATED DAYS	AVG RATING
Preferential Classroom Placement	24	▦
Proximity Control	24	▦

OBJECTIVE

	DAYS	0	1	2
Remained in assigned area	24	16.7%	33.3%	50.0%
Was quiet during assigned times	24	12.5%	41.7%	45.8%

TARGETED

	SCORED DAYS	TOTAL FREQUENCY
Out of seat at inappropriate times	11	37
Talks during quiet time	12	35

INCIDENT SUMMARY

Incident Type	Consequence	Number Of Incidents
Level 1 Offense	Counseling	1
Level 1 Offense	None Assigned	2
Level 3 Offense	Demerits	1
Level 5 Offense	Social Services Referral	1
Emotional/Instructional Support	None Assigned	1

Strategy Effectiveness Key

▫	▪	▪▪	▦
Not Used	Not Effective	Somewhat Effective	Effective

Objective Color Key

0	1	2
Red	Yellow	Dark Green

© 2011 Psychological Software Solutions, Inc.   ___ END OF REPORT ___

Print   **Email Guardian**   **Close**

Figure 4.9. Sample summary report based on multiple sources of data regarding an RtI team's behavior intervention plan for a student. The report incorporates a description of the intervention as well as outcome information. (Report produced by Review360 software, from Psychological Software Solutions Inc.)

Outcomes Assessment

Outcomes assessment is an ongoing data collection process for measuring student learning. One type of outcomes assessment is a public school's benchmark assessments, which often are aligned with high-stakes, state-mandated assessments. The district designs curriculum and instruction that meet state standards and expectations for all learners, sets appropriate criteria for the quality of student learning, systematically gathers data and provides rubrics for interpretation, and sets performance standards. Staff use these outcomes assessment data to determine how well student performance matches the expectations set forth by the state, as well as to document, explain, and improve individual student performance.

Teachers also gather ongoing outcomes data in the form of summative evaluations. The purpose of summative assessment is to inform teachers and the RtI team of what the student has learned *over time*. A summative assessment tells staff *what* to teach but not *how* to teach. Educational determinations that are often aligned with summative assessments include whether students have achieved mastery in skills taught, campus accountability for student progress(adequate yearly progress), and resource allocation. The most common types of summative assessments are end-of-chapter exams, semester final exams, high-stakes state tests (see table 4.2 for an example), and college entrance exams.

Behavior

Behavioral assessment begins with universal screening practices for academics and behavior. Student academic progress is monitored through a systematic approach to screening for grade-level performance. Universal behavioral screening investigates whether students may be having adjustment problems. The results of behav-

Table 4.2. Sample documentation of the results of a high-stakes state test

Assessment: TAKS (Texas Assessment of Knowledge and Skills) Date Administered: Spring 2010 Grade: 8	Score	Met standard?
Reading	710	Yes
Math	670	No
Math	674	No
Science	1950	No
Social studies	2240	Yes

ioral screening help teachers gain an awareness of social and emotional factors that may be affecting the student's ability to learn and to meet school expectations. Elementary students should screened yearly in the fall by the campus counselor (usually sometime in September or October). For middle school students, universal screening begins during the spring of the fifth-grade year and is also administered in October for the seventh and eight grades. High school students are screened in the spring of the eighth-grade year. A three-stage multiple-gate system is used in screening for behavior problems. Externalizing and internalizing dimensions are examined within norm-referenced screeners.

Documentation of universal screening begins with a team review of campus office discipline referrals and the identification of students who have received five or more referrals in one semester for high-intensity behaviors. Next, the team documents its review of nominations from teachers (once a year) of students who have evidenced behavioral problems in the classroom. Documentation increases to include norm-referenced behavioral screeners completed by parents and teachers. After these three phases are finished, the appropriate documentation for each student is placed in the file that the assigned case facilitator maintains on the student.

The assessment and documentation of Tier 1 positive behavior supports are also critical. The assessment is designed to focus on building and campus characteristics and practices that support student behavior preventively and proactively. Therefore the campus RtI team should collect data on the implementation of sound positive behavior support strategies in this area, such the following:

- ✔ Rules are clearly posted in classrooms and common areas throughout the buildings.
- ✔ Student feedback is given frequently.
- ✔ Positive and negative consequences for behavior are clear, consistent, immediately given, and linked to the behaviors.
- ✔ Social skills are introduced intentionally and are modeled and reinforced by all staff.
- ✔ Learning areas are neat and well organized.
- ✔ Class schedules and routines are followed consistently.
- ✔ Teacher expectations are clearly understood and intentionally taught.
- ✔ Discipline procedures are enforced in a firm and fair manner. (The number of office discipline referrals can be used as quantitative data.)

Behavioral documentation intensifies as behavioral interventions intensify, moving from the whole school and whole class to the individual student. The best method for collecting and documenting behavioral data is a functional behavioral assessment. A functional behavioral assessment is a data collection system to identify and measure problematic behaviors in terms of the student's interaction with the environment. Data are collected to describe the underlying functions of the student's behavior, analyze the triggers of the behaviors of concern, and determine the consequences that may maintain and/or extinguish those behaviors.

Direct assessments of problematic behaviors are also very helpful in data documentation. The most common direct assessment techniques used in schools are as follows (Ogonosky and Mintsioulis 2010):

Frequency—A simple count of how many times a behavior occurs during a designated period of time
- Frequency counts can be made by the minute, hour, day, or week.
- Frequency counts are most useful with behaviors that are discrete and short in duration, such as number of curse words or number of completed math problems.

Duration—The percentage of time or the total time in which a behavior occurs during a specified observation period.
- To calculate the percentage of time, add the amounts of the times (durations) in which the behavior occurred and divide the sum by the total observation period.
- Duration counts are used to track behaviors that last for more than a few seconds and for varying lengths of time, such as time on task, time spent tapping a pencil, or in-seat behavior.

Interval—A shortcut for estimating the duration of a behavior.
- An observer periodically observes the student at predetermined intervals and records whether a behavior occurs during the interval.
- There are three types of interval recording:

    - *Whole interval:* The student is observed for a few seconds at designated intervals, and the behavior is documented if it occurs during the complete observation period.
    - *Partial interval:* The student is observed for a short period, and the behavior is documented if it occurs at least once.
    - *Momentary time sampling:* At predetermined points within the observation period (e.g., 5- or 10-second interval points), the observer documents the absence or presence of the behavior at that precise moment.

Use of Multiple Sources of Data

Within the school assessment system, expectations must be high that multiple data sources will be used in problem solving for student success. This climate of expectations starts with a district vision or mission plan that clearly supports data-based decisions that are made routinely, consistently, and effectively. To provide a vehicle for its vision of reliance on data, the district should develop and maintain high-quality data systems that enable all teachers and administrators access to the data in a timely fashion. According to Mieles and Foley (2005), a strong data system is comprehensive and integrated and links multiple sources of data for reporting and analysis to a range of audiences. Therefore, teachers who have access to the data system are more likely to support the district's vision for aggregating and presenting state and district data for analysis.

However, simply giving teachers access to state and district data is not enough. Teachers must also maintain documentation of classroom-based data (formative assessments, summative assessments, and student work samples). Often this is done using traditional grade book documentation. More recently districts have been using online grade books, which easily allow teachers to prepare aggregate assessment data on student progress, content area addressed (skills aligned to lesson plan objective), or task completion. These data can then be used for identifying patterns in students' grade-level access and in outcomes related to student interaction with curriculum and instruction. Such patterns can serve as a starting point in documenting the identification of students whose classwork performance is inconsistent with their peer grade-level performance. Recall that this is the type of data used to determine whether at least 80 percent of students are achieving grade-level success within the general education classroom. Fiarman (2007) and Halverson, Prichett, and Watson (2007) recommend that analysis of multiple sources of data be conducted during teacher collaboration and planning times.

Clearly, an efficient district-wide data aggregation system is vital for thorough documentation of multiple sources of data. It is also very important that RtI assessment documentation of the struggling learner demonstrate an increase in frequency and intensity as greater student needs are revealed and interventions are intensified. Multiple reliable assessments are used in the RtI team problem-solving process to determine which students are falling behind in critical skills and need learning support. The team's documentation of use of these assessments—in consultation with the teacher—to design differentiated instruction aligned to the student's learning needs is done with a brief case facilitator form (see appendix C). Next, the team notes should examine progress-monitoring records that document the student's academic and behavioral growth, as well as diagnostics data about the foundational skills that are the essential focus of intervention. These data can be easily summed up in the RtI team meeting minutes, and any assessment data can be attached to the minutes. (For an example of a completed team meeting form for use in Tiers 2 and 3, see pages 57–59.)

It is crucial that multiple data sources be aligned so that they clearly tell the same story and that teachers use them effectively. To establish that all staff know how to use the multiple data sources, there must be documentation of professional development, confirming that teachers were trained in the district's system for aggregating data sources. Documenting the number of times the RtI team meets to analyze data can also easily be done by including the weekly team meetings on the published campus calendar and by collecting the team meeting agendas. Principals can keep a copy of this calendar (with corresponding agendas) in their RtI documentation file. Additionally, team meeting minutes should reflect the problem-solving strategies used when reviewing school-wide, classroom, and individual learner assessment data.

Chapter 5

Documenting Interventions

R tI is successful when district and campus infrastructures support strategies and interventions that result in positive outcomes for students. In addition to a strong infrastructure, teachers will require the assistance of building administrators and district staff in order to implement interventions effectively. This support of teachers must encompass not only the implementation of interventions but also the collection of appropriate data that describe the usefulness of those interventions. The RtI team's use of historical data and multiple sources of assessment when problem-solving to connect the learner to the right intervention must also be documented.

The worst-case scenario in the RtI problem-solving model occurs when a student moves through the tiers of increasing interventions, is referred for a special education assessment, and does not meet disability eligibility criteria. Such a situation is likely to spark a disagreement between parents, general education teachers, and special education staff regarding the appropriate intervention for the student. A rift may form between those who believe that special education is the only answer and those who think that the solution lies within the curriculum and delivery of instruction. But in reality the most likely reason for the student's lack of response to the interventions is a lack of integrity in the intervention selection process. The success of an intervention relies on the effective use of assessment data to design the right instructional skill match for the student, with a suitable margin of challenge (at the instructional level of the student) and consistency of implementation. The desired outcome of an RtI plan is a sustained pattern of growth, indicating a narrowing of the grade-level achievement gap for the student. A behavioral intervention is considered successful when there is a reduction in the problem behavior and/or an increase in the desired replacement behavior.

Tier 1: Core Curriculum and Instruction

When a student begins to evidence academic or behavioral issues that decrease academic engagement time or grade-level success, the RtI team assigns a collaborator (case facilitator) to consult with the student's teacher in selecting and implementing evidence-based instructional and/or behavioral strategies. To meet the individual needs of the struggling learner, the interventions selected must align with related assessment data. According to Witt, VanDerHeyden, and Gilbertson (2004), this process begins with a clear definition of the identified problem(s). It is imperative that the problem definition be honed to no more than two concerns. The teacher identifies the top two issues that are interfering with the student's ability to interact with the curriculum and instruction. Documenting the problems concisely and in quantifiable terms is extremely important for selecting an appropriate intervention and monitoring its effectiveness. This process begins with Tier 1 instructional strategies and core curriculum supports, which should be documented in the case facilitator's follow-up documentation (see page 50). The types of data that the teacher and the case facilitator review together include the following:

✔ Universal screening data
✔ The core instructional scope and lesson plan sequence, within a scientifically validated curriculum that meets state standards
✔ Copies of student products and assessments for analysis of the student's skill weaknesses to be targeted
✔ Types of instructional adjustments currently being used in the classroom with all students through whole-class and small-group differentiated instruction
✔ Examples of differentiated content, process, and products used with the student of concern
✔ Comparison of the student's grade-level skills with those of peers

Next, the case facilitator documents the formative and summative assessments collected by the teacher that will be used to track the intervention's effectiveness. Progress monitoring using curriculum-based measurement or other forms of weekly assessments can also be used as documentation in Tier 1. The remaining intervention documentation should be in the form of lesson plans that conform to state standards, flexible class grouping with differentiated student products, and any type of scheduled core curriculum support given to the student for grade-level success (such as tutoring). Tier 1 documentation is not so much about filling out a required form; rather, it focuses on the differentiated student products aligned with lesson plans and student learning style. The connection of a student's preferred learning style to instructional grouping and differentiated products is very important to document. Therefore the campus staff may want to select a learning style inventory to be used whenever a team decides to monitor a student in Tier 1.

Although having a campus or district documentation form is helpful for planning an RtI intervention, it is insufficient as the sole means of documenting the intervention process. The RtI team should collect evidence-based techniques for differentiation of content and strategic interventions and make them available to teachers through an RtI resource library or tool kit. One resource for selecting interventions for a variety of content areas, including both mathematics and reading, is the What Works Clearinghouse (http://ies.ed.gov/ncee/wwc/), which was established in 2002 by the U.S. Department of Education's Institute of Education Sciences to provide school personnel with scientific evidence of what works in education.

In addition to naturally occurring data and products within the context of the general education class, the intervention documentation at Tier 1 should include elements related to the case facilitator's contributions. It is recommended that the district establish case facilitator responsibilities in its RtI guidelines, so that expectations and the communication between staff, parents, and RtI team members are clear. For examples of Tier 1 documentation for case facilitators, see pages 49 and 50.

Tier 1 documentation does not end when the intensity of interventions increases as a student moves into Tier 2. Tier 1 data collection and consultation continue throughout the entire process of RtI. Useful forms for documenting Tier 1 interventions in specific subject areas are included in appendix D (see pages 101–104).

Tiers 2 and 3: Strategic Interventions

Tier 2 intervention documentation begins with the official Tier 2 entry-point meeting that verifies the need for increased intervention intensity and describes the intervention that will be initiated and monitored. The documentation should also include who was invited to the meeting, each person's role on the team, and the required data that were brought to the team meeting. A sample completed Notification of Tier 2 RtI Team Meeting form appears on page 51. For continuity of documentation, this same form may be to document Tier 3 meetings as well.

Who may be invited to the meeting?

✔ Campus administrator
✔ Parents
✔ General education teachers

RtI Documentation: Problem Specification Checklist for Tier 1 Case Facilitator Initial Consultation

(Limit to 2 primary areas.)

Student: _Carrie Dunn_____ Teacher: _Ms. Smith_____

Case Facilitator: _Steven Alvarado_____ Return by: _1/9/11_____

Academic Readiness   **Language**
_____Recall of personal information   _____Expressive language
_____Shape recognition   _____Receptive language
_____Color recognition
_____1:1 correspondence
_____Number identification
_____Uppercase letter identification
_____Lowercase letter identification
_____Counting
_____Recitation of alphabet
_____Other areas: _____ _____

Reading   **Math**
_____Pre-literacy skills   _____Quantity
      Specify: _____Number recognition
                                                 _____Number concepts
                                                 _____Calculation accuracy
                                                 _____Applications
_____Sight words   _____Word problems
__X__Fluency: (accuracy and quickness)   _____Measurement
__X__Vocabulary development   _____Pre-algebra concepts
_____Comprehension   _____Math vocabulary

Writing
_____Fine motor or handwriting
_____Conventions (punctuation, capitalization)
_____Language (sentence structure, grammar, vocabulary)
_____Construction of story (prose, action, sequence, theme)
_____Fluency
_____Spelling

Behavior
Description (type, frequency, duration, setting):
   Carrie does not evidence any problem behaviors at school. She is polite and works hard
   despite her measured difficulties with reading fluency.
_____
_____
_____
_____

Please complete and return to the RtI team after initial teacher consultation.

RtI Documentation: Tier 1 Case Facilitator Follow-up

Student:__Carrie Dunn_____ Teacher:__Ms. Smith_____

Case Facilitator:__Steven Alvarado_____ Initial Contact Date:___1/12/11_____

Week____1____**Tier**___1___

Are the interventions being implemented as designed?   Ⓨ/ N

If not, why not?__Ms. Smith used additional instructional supports within a flexible grouping___
where Carrie practiced reading fluency at grade level with material of her choice from the library.

Are additional supports/resources needed?
_None at this time._____

_____

What is intervention outcome? Was there a response to intervention?   Ⓨ/ N

Carrie had an increase of 3 words correct per min. on timed oral reading passages, a slight increase
in fluency after 1 week additional practice in a small-group setting during independent seatwork.

Have there been classroom observations for fidelity?   Y /Ⓝ   Fidelity check is scheduled for
   week 3; however, a review of student work samples show additional differentiation of content
   delivery by seating her closer to the word wall, as designated by her learning style inventory.

Have there been classroom observations for documentation of curriculum, learner, and
environmental variables?   Ⓨ/ N

Week____2____**Tier**___1___

Are the interventions being implemented as designed?   Y /Ⓝ

If not, why not?__Ms. Smith was out ill for 3 days._____

_____

Are additional supports/resources needed?
Ms. Smith is designing appropriate work for Carrie to be included in her lesson plans in the event
_that she is absent again during the intervention process._____

What is intervention outcome? Was there a response to intervention?   Y / N
_This could not be determined due to lack of intervention fidelity._____

_____

Have there been classroom observations for fidelity?   Y /Ⓝ

Have there been classroom observations for documentation of curriculum, learner, and
environmental variables?   Y / N

Week____3___**Tier**___1___

Are the interventions being implemented as designed?   Ⓨ/ N

If not, why not?_____

_____

Are additional supports/resources needed?
Ms. Smith would like reading coach to visit classroom and provide additional reading materials
for fluency practice. Contacted coach on 2/7/11; scheduled planning time for 2/9/11 at 9:00 a.m.

What is intervention outcome? Was there a response to intervention?   Ⓨ/ N
But increase was minimal; rate increased only an additional 2 words correct per minute.

_____

Have there been classroom observations for fidelity?   Y / N

Have there been classroom observations for documentation of curriculum, learner, and
environmental variables?   Y / N

Notification of Tier 2 RtI Team Meeting

To: _Mr. and Mrs. Dunn, Steven Alvarado, Ms. Smith, RtI team members_   Date: _3/1/11_

Purpose: RtI team meeting to discuss Tier 1 interventions and progress. Please be prepared to present documentation of curriculum, instruction, interventions, and any other data you have collected on the following child to the RtI team.

Student: _Carrie Dunn_   Grade: __3__

Please bring copies of the following, as applicable. Check off each item as it is filed:

_____Documentation of Tier 1 Instruction and Interventions form
_____Attendance records
_____Health screening
_____Multiple intelligence Learning profile
_____Grades printout
_____Photocopies of all standardized and criterion-referenced tests/assessment data
_____ARI/AMI/title documentation
_____Lesson plans
_____Student work samples (e.g, journal, spelling tests, math computation)
_____Discipline record printout
_____Any other documentation that shows Tier 1 classroom interventions
_____Home Language Survey
_____Parent conference documentation

If you have any questions, please contact an RtI team member before your assigned time.

Thank you,

_____
RtI Team Chair

✔ Counselors

✔ Instructional coaches

✔ School psychologists

✔ Student services personnel (including various types of intervention specialists)

✔ Special education teachers

✔ The student (when appropriate)

When the team formally convenes a meeting regarding the intensified intervention, several agenda items are to be discussed and documented. The documentation of this meeting should focus on the purpose of the problem solving and the solutions that the team determines are necessary for student growth. Specifically, the documentation will describe the following:

✔ The RtI individual student plan, which includes targeted content and strategic instruction aligned with foundational skill weaknesses in the targeted content area

✔ The interventionist assigned

✔ Intensity of the intervention (e.g., 30 minutes, 2 times per week)

✔ Individual assessments to be used (such as progress monitoring, diagnostics, etc.)

✔ Length of intervention period (e.g., 6 weeks)

✔ Date of scheduled follow-up meeting

It is important for the RtI team to demonstrate purposeful, thoughtful planning and problem solving in the team meeting documentation. The following items need to be clearly and concisely documented:

1. *Problem identification*—The student's needs must be described in quantifiable terms. This entry point into planning for intensified intervention is usually completed by the case facilitator, who reviews multiple data sources to hone in on the student's problem areas. The following are examples of the data sources whose information should be reflected on the case facilitator's documentation forms (see pages 49 and 50) and aligned with the RtI team meeting documentation form used in Tiers 2 and 3 (see page 58):

   ✔ Completed copies of Tier 1 instructional strategies used by the teachers, along with matching student products

   ✔ Any documentation gathered when implementing core curriculum support, such as tutoring (concepts covered, dates of sessions)

✔ Documentation of academic engagement activities

✔ A copy of the student's learning style inventory

✔ Student work samples

✔ Teacher lesson plans with review documentation

✔ Assessment (formative, summative, and common assessments; district benchmarks; progress monitoring)

✔ Attendance and tardy information

✔ Contacts with parents

✔ Parent-teacher conferences

2. ***Inventory of student strengths and talents***—By taking stock of a student's strengths, the team may be able to identify skills that are important to the overall success of the plan. The team should discuss and document the student's strengths as well as any incentives that are known to increase the student's motivation. This information is valuable when creating an intervention plan that motivates the student to achieve success.

   Example:

   La-Tricia has excellent fine motor skills, as evidenced in her ability to draw intricate patterns of art. She enjoys any type of art activities, works very well with hands-on manipulatives, and responds very well to teacher attention.

3. ***Student health or other variables***—Sometimes physical or health issues, such as vision or hearing problems, may be affecting the student's ability to learn. Such factors need to be addressed and documented in order to provide the correct instructional strategy.

4. ***Selection of targeted areas for intervention***—The top two areas of concern are selected on the basis of interviews with the teacher and the parents and multiple sources of assessment. These concerns must be described in a quantifiable manner. Behavioral concerns are discussed and documented in terms of frequency, intensity, and/or duration of the challenging behavior. For academic concerns, documentation should record the presence of the underlying academic skill deficits, mismatch between student skills and classroom instruction (as evidenced by lesson plans), fluency and accuracy rates, comprehension or higher-level strategy deficits, and problems regarding classwork or homework completion.

Example:

James demonstrates difficulty decoding words in first-grade text. He currently reads 12 words correct per minute from a first-grade passage, whereas his peers are currently reading 42 words correct per minute from a second-grade passage. His fluency rate affects his work completion rate, as James has completed only 1 of his last 5 reading assignments.

Not this:

James is reading poorly. He cannot keep up with his classmates and becomes frustrated.

5. ***Baseline data review and goal setting***—Discuss and document baseline data collected for the targeted concern(s), whether academic or behavioral. Again, the measures used will be fluency rate for academics and frequency, intensity, and/or duration for behavior. For academics, the baseline data point is determined by using a curriculum-based measure. Once the baseline data are recorded, the team sets an outcome goal. *It is recommended that the district provide guidelines for outcome goal setting, in order to ensure consistency in this process.* Outcome goals should be reasonable, using research-based learning rates as a foundation. The goals for improvement should be stated in terms of 6 to 12 weeks.

Example:

James's baseline is 10 words correct per minute on a fluency probe with an instructional reading level 1.5. The outcome goal is that James will increase his learning rate by 2 words correct per minute each week over a 12-week period. At the end of 12 weeks the expected outcome goal for rate of improvement is 34 words correct per minute on a fluency probe with an instructional level 1.5.

6. ***Design of the intervention plan***—After a review of the various forms of student data, the RtI team will have a good idea of why the student is having difficulty learning. This is known as a hypothesis and becomes the focal point for intervention design. It is critical that the hypothesis statement conforms with all of the data collected so far.

Example:

James's reading is affected by his slow rate of decoding, as noted in his in class assessments, common assessments, diagnostic assessments, and curriculum-based measures.

Next, the team decides on an intervention that aligns with the hypothesis.

Example:

Since James is demonstrating difficulty decoding, he needs a reading intervention that provides additional strategic and explicit instruction on alphabetic understanding and phonemic awareness.

Once the documentation of the hypothesis and the strategic intervention is entered on the team meeting documentation form (page 57), the team should discuss and record the following particulars of the intervention:

a. *When and where the intervention will occur.* (Example: Tuesdays, Wednesdays, and Thursdays at 1:00–1:30 p.m. in the library learning center.)

b. *Length of intervention time.* The length of time that the intervention is to be implemented must be documented. Monitoring of student progress typically is done in periods of 6 to 12 weeks. However, the length of the period may vary according to publisher recommendations, student attendance, or research data on the specific interventions selected. Determining an appropriate length of time for intervention implementation is a very important part of the decision-making and documentation process because an insufficient implementation time may yield a false negative in the data, indicating minimal student learning. On the other hand, too much time spent on an intervention that is not working may delay the team's development of more-effective instruction and intervention for the student. One avenue for protecting against these errors is to make sure the interventionist is frequently monitoring student progress and continuously relaying this information to the teacher and the case facilitator.

c. *Any specialized materials or training required to implement the interventions.* (Example: specialized reading program, such as Lexia Learning.)

d. *Who will implement the intervention.* (Example: campus reading coach.)

e. *Methods for monitoring intervention fidelity.* (Example: administrator observation using fidelity check, student attendance sheet.)

7. **Method of progress monitoring**—Team meeting notes should indicate the person(s) responsible for the progress monitoring, which assessments will be used, where the progress monitoring will take place, and what types of fidelity checks will be used.

Example:

James will be progress-monitored using district-designed first-grade oral reading fluency passages. His progress monitoring will be conducted by the campus reading coach at the end of his reading intervention sessions every Tuesday and Thursday. Fidelity checks for assessment will be conducted weekly by the case facilitator, who will review progress-monitoring passages and graphs.

8. ***Parent communication plan***—The team meeting form should include a record of who is responsible for communicating with parents regarding student progress at both the grade level (Tier 1) and the instructional level (supplemental intervention in Tier 2 or 3). The team also documents the times designated for parent contact.

   Example:

   James's teacher, Ms. Smith, will contact his parents weekly with updates regarding his grade-level progress and will document these contacts on a parent communication log. The case facilitator will contact the parents bimonthly with progress-monitoring updates for the duration of the intervention and will document these contacts.

9. ***Review and approval of the RtI plan***—The final phase of documenting the problem-solving process is for the team to review the proposed RtI plan and to record that all team members are in agreement with it. Then a date is selected for a follow-up meeting. This date typically is 6 weeks after the initiation of the intervention, but the timing of the follow-up meeting will vary according to the intervention selected and student progress.

10. ***Participation log***—It is important to conclude the documentation of the team meeting by having all meeting participants sign a sheet that indicates their participation in the meeting and the plan design.

One of the most important aspects of data collection in Tiers 2 and 3 is that the data be described in a manner that allows staff to evaluate whether the instructional strategies and interventions are effective. A great way to accomplish this at the follow-up review meeting is to provide the team with a snapshot of the ongoing assessment (see the sample form on page 62). The learning history of a student within an RtI system is easily recorded by ensuring that the RtI process and its documentation incorporate these elements:

Documentation of Tier 2/Tier 3 RtI Team Meeting

Student: Carrie Dunn   Teacher: Ms. Smith

Case Facilitator: Steven Alvarado   Date of Meeting: 3/15/11

Step 1: Problem Identification

- Tier 1 Instructional strategies used and student outcomes
- Core curriculum support documentation
- Academic engagement strategies documentation
- Student multiple intelligence profiles and learning inventories
- Student work samples
- Lesson plans/schedules
- Assessments (including but not limited to fluency probes, common assessments, and district benchmarks)
- Additional Tier 1 strategies used
- Any additional data (e.g., attendance and tardy records, parent contacts, conferences)

Step 2: Inventory of Student Strengths and Talents

Carrie is very gifted in math and math problem solving. She enjoys solving equations and is quick to help others during math independent practice. Carrie enjoys teacher praise. She is involved in Girl Scouts and has many friends.

Step 3: Health and Other Variables Affecting Learning

Documentation indicates:

Carrie wears corrective lenses. Her vision is 20/40, but corrected. She always wears her glasses to school. All other health records are normal.

Step 4: Selection of Targeted Areas of Intervention

List two targeted concerns:

1. Reading fluency _____

2. Vocabulary development _____

Note: Add these concerns to the Targeted Area of Instruction section on the Documentation of Tier 2 or 3 Intervention and Assessment form.

Step 5: Baseline Data Review and Goal Setting

Content area: __Developmental reading_____ Instructional level: __1.0_____

Goals (expected weekly growth and number of intervention weeks):

The team expects Carrie's weekly rate of growth in oral reading fluency to be 2 additional words read correctly per minute each week.

Step 6: Design of Intervention Plan

Hypothesis statement: __Carrie lacks developmental fluency and vocabulary skills, and this is__ __affecting her ability to read at third grade level.__

Strategic intervention(s) identified: __Continued Tier 1 supports with flexible grouping, lesson__ __plan differentiation, and tutorials. Added strategic reading instruction using Lexia Learning__ __software for 30 minutes, 3 times per week.__

Where: __Library learning lab_____

When: __Monday, Wednesday, Friday, 9:00–9:30 a.m._____

Resources needed: __Computer, Lexia Learning software__

Interventionist assigned: __Reading coach_____

Data collector (progress monitoring): __Reading coach_____

Step 7: Method of Progress Monitoring

Data collector: __Reading coach_____

Where: __Library learning lab_____

When: __Monday and Friday, end of intervention period_____

Fidelity check (date): __4/6/11_____

Step 8: Parent Communication Plan

Parent contact: Steven Alvarado and Ms. Smith

Time: Steven Alvarado, every 2 weeks; Ms. Smith, weekly

Step 9: Intervention and Monitoring Review

Members in agreement?   X Yes   ___ No

Follow-up meeting date: 4/25/11

Case manager consultation follow-up date: 3/29/11

Step 10: Signature record *(All members in attendance sign.)*

Name	Position
	Chairperson
	Teacher of Record
	Case Manager
	Timekeeper
	Data Manager
	Scribe
	Interventionist
	Team Member
	Team Member
	Parent

✔ Clearly defined components of a multi-tier instruction and intervention system

✔ Clearly articulated rules and procedures for making decisions regarding student movement between tiers

✔ High integrity of intervention implementation

✔ Continuous data collection, with increasing intensity across all tiers

✔ Purposeful examination of data by the problem-solving team to determine whether increasingly intensive support is needed

✔ Assessment documentation of any significant discrepancy in the level of a student's performance relative to that of peers and to state standards

✔ Assessment documentation of any significant discrepancy in a student's rate of progress relative to that of peers when provided with high-quality interventions implemented over time

If a student continues to display difficulty learning despite intensified interventions, the team may want to consider a referral for special education evaluation. Child Find responsibilities for school districts kick in whenever there is a suspicion that the student has a disability and needs special education programming. Data collection within the tiers should be able to substantiate this suspicion. According to Martin (2010), campus personnel need to address the following questions:

✔ Is there a time during the RtI process when the problem-solving team suspects that a potential learning disability exists?

✔ What is the appropriate length of intervention time without learning rate progress that is sufficient for a referral for special education evaluation to occur?

✔ What should a team do with respect to Child Find if the student is receiving intensified interventions and showing some improvement, but still demonstrates deficits in a specific achievement area?

✔ How can campus teams avoid failure-to-identify claims while attempting to use the RtI process appropriately prior to referral?

The most effective way to answer these and similar questions is to align the RtI process with the district's special education referral process. For guidance with regard to the documentation required for a strong special education referral (based on IDEA 2004), see the sample rubric presented in table 5.1 (page 63).

• • •

Documenting the effectiveness of the intervention phase of the RtI problem-solving process is critical for student success. This documentation serves as the campus team's description of its plan for a student, as well as the student's response. The documentation must present a clear picture of the integrity of both the decision-making process and the intervention implementation. If that has been accomplished, the steps taken by staff to support the struggling learner will be obvious to a reader of the documentation. The documented data are also extremely important if a Child Find issue should result in a referral for Section 504 or special education evaluation. If all data collected are aligned accurately and documented concisely, there is less chance that disputes (professional or legal) will arise regarding the appropriate educational supports a struggling learner needs to achieve academic success.

RtI Documentation: Tier 2/Tier 3 Intervention and Assessment

Interventionist: Reading coach   Student: Carrie Dunn   Grade: 3   Tier: 1

Instructional Skill(s)/Level	Date	Day of Week	No. of Minutes	Progress-Monitoring Data
Fluency building using district-developed fluency practice support, instructional level 2. See attached diagnostics.	1/31/11	Ⓜ T W Th F		CBM probe level 1.0 DCPM WCPM 30 BCPM
Fluency building using district-developed fluency practice support, instructional level 2. See attached diagnostics.	2/2/11	M T Ⓦ Th F		CBM probe level 1.0 DCPM WCPM 32 BCPM
Fluency building using district-developed fluency practice support, instructional level 2. See attached diagnostics.	2/7/11	Ⓜ T W Th F		CBM probe level 1.0 DCPM WCPM 30 BCPM
Additional practice materials aligned with attached lesson plan provided during activity-period tutorials. (See attached.)	2/9/11	M T Ⓦ Th F		CBM probe level 1.0 DCPM WCPM 30 BCPM
		M T W Th F		CBM probe level DCPM WCPM BCPM
		M T W Th F		CBM probe level DCPM WCPM BCPM
		M T W Th F		CBM probe level DCPM WCPM BCPM
		M T W Th F		CBM probe level DCPM WCPM BCPM
		M T W Th F		CBM probe level DCPM WCPM BCPM
		M T W Th F		CBM probe level DCPM WCPM BCPM
		M T W Th F		CBM probe level DCPM WCPM BCPM
		M T W Th F		CBM probe level DCPM WCPM BCPM

Abbreviations: WCPM, words correct per minute; DCPM, digits correct per minute; BCPM, behaviors correct per minute.

Table 5.1. Necessary documentation to support special education referral and eligibility decisions

Special education eligibility criteria	Supporting documentation
The child does not achieve adequately for the child's age or to meet state-approved grade-level standards in one or more of the following areas, when provided with learning experiences and instruction appropriate for the child's age or state-approved grade-level standards: ✔ Oral expression ✔ Listening comprehension ✔ Written expression ✔ Basic reading skills ✔ Reading fluency skills ✔ Reading comprehension ✔ Mathematics calculation ✔ Mathematics problem solving	✔ Universal screening ✔ District benchmark data ✔ Formative assessments ✔ Summative assessments ✔ Common assessments ✔ Student work samples
The child does not make sufficient progress to meet age or state-approved grade-level standards in one or more of the areas identified in 34 CFR 300.309(a)(1) when using a process based on the child's response to scientific, research-based intervention.	Data documentation records for ✔ Tiers 1–3 to include the following: ✔ Universal screening ✔ Diagnostic assessments ✔ Progress monitoring ✔ All formative and summative assessments ✔ Case facilitator notes ✔ Team meeting documentation
To ensure that underachievement in a child suspected of having a specific learning disability is not due to lack of appropriate instruction in reading or math, the group must consider, as part of the evaluation described in 34 CFR 300.304 through 300.306: ✔ Data that demonstrate that prior to, or as a part of, the referral process, the child was provided appropriate instruction in regular education settings, delivered by qualified personnel; and ✔ Data-based documentation of repeated assessments of achievement at reasonable intervals, reflecting formal assessment of student progress during instruction, which was provided to the child's parents.	✔ Teacher lesson plans ✔ Team review of lesson plans ✔ Attendance records ✔ Student work samples designed to differentiate students needs ✔ Documentation of staff training

Chapter 6

Documenting Fidelity

According to Gresham et al. (2000), fidelity for RtI purposes is providing instruction in the way it was designed to be delivered. The goal of fidelity is to assure the integrity of assessment, instruction, and the RtI process throughout all of the tiers. The implementation of the fidelity aspect of RtI can be difficult and emotional and thus may have an impact on how well documentation occurs. Documentation of fidelity sometimes makes staff feel vulnerable, resulting in reactivity and distrust. Change in habits and routines is difficult, and the fidelity component of RtI documentation often brings about change in a school's climate and culture. Veteran educators may have a routine for how they develop lesson plans and teach, and when that routine is monitored or questioned, discomfort may follow and barriers to documentation may arise. Nevertheless, within the RtI process, Tier 1 documentation of instructional fidelity is the foundation that sustains Tier 2 and Tier 3 interventions. Quite simply, Tier 1 fidelity must be in place in order for Tier 2 and Tier 3 interventions to be successful.

Documenting fidelity can be done through a variety of means: use of checklists, peer feedback (grade-level and content-area teams), case facilitator follow-up, and direct observations. The premise of RtI is to be proactive and preventive; therefore the best way to ensure fidelity is to be proactive and to produce documentation that supports the proactive measures taken. According to the National Center on Response to Intervention (2011), detailed preparations for an RtI framework that increases fidelity include the following steps:

✔ Clearly describe RtI procedures, systems, and components (in a district/campus guidance document aligned with state guidelines).
✔ Succinctly define the responsibilities of staff and team members.
✔ Create a data system for measuring RtI procedures, systems, and components.
✔ Link instruction and interventions to improved outcomes (via continuous review of multiple sources of data).
✔ Create a consistent system for providing feedback and making decisions.
✔ Create accountability measures for noncompliance to be used when necessary.

Fidelity is also the means for ensuring that students have appropriate access to instruction, assessment, and intervention. Although fidelity is a simple concept, it is the most difficult to implement and document. Documentation of fidelity is based on collected data and ensures that all of the components necessary for integrity of the student's curriculum, instruction, environment, and individualized RtI plan are present. Therefore documentation of fidelity should focus on four distinct areas:

1. Core curriculum and instruction
2. Assessments
3. Interventions
4. Team process

The campus administrator is the person primarily responsible for upholding fidelity and should discuss this aspect of the documentation at each RtI meeting held for the student.

Because fidelity is an integral part of each of the four areas of the district RtI process, *it is unwise to create extra documentation when it is not needed.* Too often RtI paperwork is unnecessarily cumbersome, and the additional time teachers spend on it takes away from instruction. Use of data collection throughout the four areas can serve more than one purpose; therefore, *whenever possible, use already-collected data to support fidelity documentation.*

Core Curriculum and Instruction

Within the RtI process, Tier 1 fidelity functions as the foundation on which Tier 2 and Tier 3 interventions are built. Simply put, Tier 1 fidelity must be in place if intervention in Tiers 2 and 3 are to be successful. The integrity of the curriculum and delivery of instruction lies in the classroom teacher's background knowledge and training, with support from the grade-level and content-area teams. To ensure the integrity of instructional delivery, teachers must be consistent in differentiating and delivering the curriculum according to how it was designed and validated through research.

The first step in ensuring curriculum and instruction fidelity is to simply review the district's curriculum framework and provide the resources necessary for its implementation by teachers. This is typically done by the district level RtI team and district curriculum specialist. Next, documentation of continuous staff development linked to district-wide data reviews is important; this particular type of documentation is carried out three times a year during the RtI team reviews of universal screening data, using the Tier 1 problem-solving documentation form discussed in chapter 4 (page 34). A good way to ensure that Tier 1 strategies and differentiation continue to be implemented is to have a case facilitator visit regularly scheduled team meetings as necessary when an individual student is receiving Tier 2 or Tier 3 strategic interventions. This practice can be documented on the Tier 1 case facilitator follow-up documentation form discussed in chapter 5 (page 50).

Many naturally occurring types of data collection can also be used for reviewing the fidelity of curriculum and instruction, such as copies of lesson plans, student work samples, attendance records, and office discipline referrals. It is essential that classroom observations be used to obtain classroom fidelity data. Teachers should be informed that these observations are designed not only to gather information about and document the fidelity of instruction but also to assemble information that will guide teams in supporting teachers in their quest to reach and teach all learners. Fidelity documentation thus is a way of both providing feedback for teachers and determining which resources are necessary to help them deliver high-quality instruction and interventions. At the campus RtI team meeting, a checklist, completed by the administrator, guides the discussion regarding strong instructional foundations in the classroom. An example of a completed Tier 1 fidelity checklist is shown on page 67.

When documenting behavior within Tier 1, student access to school- and campus-wide positive behavior supports needs to be documented, as does the fidelity of these supports. Other elements that are critical to include in behavioral documentation are the teaching and modeling of classroom behavioral expectations, and the effective design and management of classrooms to increase academic engagement time. All of these aspects can be documented on the case facilitator follow-up documentation form discussed in chapter 5 (page 50), the RtI Classroom Observations form discussed in chapter 3 (page 29), and the RtI fidelity checklist for Tier 1 (discussed in the previous paragraph).

Assessments

Fidelity in the data collection process means that all individuals are following exactly the same procedures when collecting data. RtI documentation should focus on the multiple sources of assessment data used throughout the problem-solving process—specifically screening, diagnostics, progress monitoring, and outcomes assessment. It is essential that all staff understand these assessment systems. Training on RtI assessment can be documented on the staff training form discussed in chapter 3 (page 23).

The fidelity of classroom formative and summative assessments, both academic and behavioral, can be documented as part of the routine collaboration and data collection done by the case facilitator and the classroom teacher. These records are

RTI Fidelity Checklist: Tier 1 Curriculum and Instruction Strategies

Student: Brandon Lee   Teacher: Ms. Smith   Grade: 6 (Language Arts)

Date and Time: 3/11/11, 10 a.m.   Class Size: 19   Observer: A. Ogonosky

Grouping: __X__ Whole-Class Instruction   _____ Small Group   __X__ Paired   _____ Individual (1:1)

Description of Lesson Objective: Students will use a dictionary, a glossary, or a thesaurus (printed or electronic) to determine the meanings, syllabication, pronunciations, alternate word choices, and parts of speech of words.

Specific to Core Instruction Delivery:

Yes	Sometimes	No	Not Observed	Observation Descriptor	Notes
X				Lesson plan objective is clearly communicated to students.	Listed on white board. Reading vocabulary development—(C) TEKS objective.
X				Lesson plan objectives are evident in student work samples.	Students are journaling and designing scrapbooks using multiple reference aids.
X				Teacher delivers instruction consistent with lesson plan objectives.	
X				Delivery of instruction allows time for practice of objective.	
X				Teacher has necessary resources to differentiate content, process, and product.	All students have thesaurus and dictionary available through books and technology.
X				Teacher-student interactions are positive, reinforcing strong teacher-student relationships.	Teacher is mobile; positive corrective feedback; good eye contact.
X				Teacher provides continuous constructive feedback to students.	
X				Measured academic engagement time of class is high.	All students were authentically engaged and positively interacting with teacher, curriculum, resources.

1 of 2

Specific to Differentiation of Content for Struggling Student(s):   *(Check all that are observed.)*

Cooperative Learning	Learning Environment	Student Products	Differentiation	Suggestions
___ Small group ___ Cooperative learning roles ___ Variety of criteria for grouping Other: ___	X Classroom management X Classroom organization ___ Classroom centers X Behavior rules posted ___ Student objectives posted X Reinforcing effort Other: ___	X Physical representations (models, books, etc.) ___ Musical representations ___ Poetry ___ Dramatic responses (play, role-playing, reenactment) Other: ___	X Student work samples X Presentation of material ___ Use of manipulatives ___ Classroom organization X Use of visual representations	

Multiple Intelligences	Questioning Strategies	Research-Based Strategies	Notes
___ Print—printed or written word ___ Aural—listening ___ Interactive verbalization X Visual—seeing visual descriptions such as pictures and graphs ___ Haptic—sense of touch or grasp ___ Kinesthetic—whole-body movement ___ Olfactory—smell and taste	___ Linguistic intelligence ("word smart") ___ Logical-mathematical intelligence ("number/reasoning smart") ___ Spatial intelligence ("picture smart") ___ Bodily-kinesthetic intelligence ("body smart") ___ Musical intelligence ("music smart") ___ Interpersonal intelligence ("people smart") ___ Intrapersonal intelligence ("self smart") ___ Naturalist intelligence ("nature smart")	___ Implicit vs. explicit questions ___ Higher order vs. lower order X Analytical X Reflective ___ Summarizing ___ Wait time X Modeling ___ Anchor activities ___ 4-step problem-solving approach ___ Timed drills to increase fluency ___ Use of student response cards X Graphic organizers X Vocabulary instruction ___ Self-monitoring chart ___ Homework planner	Peer modeling was used effectively, with Brandon being paired with a strong peer support for designing his scrapbook. Additionally, models of completed scrapbooks were used to aid Brandon in understanding his finished product while building his vocabulary words. He was given list of words with definitions to help him practice and use grade-level vocabulary.

then incorporated within the Tier 1 case facilitator follow-up documentation form (page 50). It is suggested that a copy of the student's assessments be attached to this form when a concern arises regarding the fidelity of the assessments. For example, if the multiple data sources reviewed by the team do not present a consistent picture of the student's strengths and weaknesses, this inconsistency could indicate a potential problem with assessment fidelity.

Curriculum-based measurement is a common assessment system that districts use for both progress monitoring (discussed in chapter 4) and universal screening. Documentation of the fidelity of this type of assessment begins a review of the diagnostic data generated, to ensure that the correct instructional level and skills are being assessed. Next, the standardized administration procedures, scheduled assessment dates, and decision making that is tied to the graphed results (determining baseline data, creating outcome goals, graphing data points, and using researched comparison norms) are examined. The best way to document the fidelity of the administration of these assessments is through direct observation. The observer should focus on six points:

1. Staff give instructions as scripted.
2. A timer is used to measure the length of administration, as designed.
3. Staff provide prompts according to researched rules.
4. Probes are scored according to scoring rubrics.
5. Graphing procedures are followed.
6. The instructional specialist relies on research-based norms or RtI problem-solving procedures to drive decisions about intervention.

Observations of the administration of curriculum-based measures occur in two contexts: during universal screening in the general education classroom and during progress monitoring of the small-group strategic intervention. Natural documentation of these assessments can serve as the primary fidelity check, with observations being made only if a concern is raised regarding the integrity of the administration of the assessments. The participants in a team meeting can easily discern whether items 4 through 6 in the above list are being implemented with fidelity.

Behavioral assessments must meet similar criteria for fidelity. The easiest way to document fidelity of the behavior assessment process is for the team to review collected behavioral data during the team meeting and verify that the correct data were gathered (as designed by the RtI behavior intervention plan) during the designated times. Fidelity is then documented in the team meeting notes (keep it simple). Sample documentation of a behavior plan that is simple but provides the framework for integrity of the process is shown in figures 4.7–4.9 in chapter 4. As discussed in Ogonosky and Mintsioulis (2010), the behavior plan itself becomes the document that drives the integrity of the behavioral intervention and assessment.

Strategic Interventions in Tiers 2 and 3

Fidelity documentation of the implementation of strategic interventions can be done easily by reviewing assessment data, attendance records, and results from observations during the intervention period. Typically districts choose to use prototypical interventions to increase consistency and efficacy of the intervention. The most important requirement of an intervention is that it has been scientifically validated. This means that the intervention is a set of research-based strategies and instruction that is implemented with small groups of students who demonstrate needs. These strategies and instruction are designed to be delivered in a scripted, systematic manner.

An intervention implementation form is a useful team tool for tracking the data being collected, thereby ensuring the integrity of the process. This form should track three aspects of intervention integrity: the date and time when the student received the intervention and assessments, the strategies and additional instruction (program) selected for the intervention, and the targeted skills (academic or behavioral) of the intervention. These forms are completed as part of the team process documentation (see samples on pages 101–104). Additionally, a simple observation during the strategic intervention time is a sound way to document fidelity. An example of documenting an observation of a strategic intervention at Tier 2 or Tier 3 is shown on page 62.

> Do not forget to monitor attendance data for interventions. If the student is not present, then the integrity of the intervention cannot be validated.

Team Process

It is critical that the RTI process be routinely assessed for fidelity. This applies not only during the initial implementation period but also as the process is institutionalized and maintained over time, in order to detect any drift from fidelity. Documenting the integrity of campus performance with regard to the RTI process is the responsibility of the RtI team members. Such documentation is necessary in order for parents and staff to trust the system and its use of data for increasing student growth. An element of accountability resonates within the documentation when staff and parents receive constructive criticism regarding the curriculum, instruction, environment, and individual learner variables involved. The best way to ensure fidelity of the campus and team processes is to use a district RtI guidance document (see appendix A for an example). This document should include strategies

RtI Fidelity Checklist: Tier 2/Tier 3 Interventions

Student: Leroy Munoz   Interventionist: Mr. Jackson   Grade: 5

Date and Time: 10/14/11, 9:30 a.m.   Observer: Ms. Field

Grouping: __X__ Small Group   _____ Paired   _____ Individual (1:1)

Description of Instructional Level Lesson Objective: Tier 2 intervention delivered by teacher using teacher guide (grade 3 instructional level) for increasing reading fluency.

Specific to Delivery of Intervention:

Yes	No	Not Observed	Observation Descriptor	Notes
		X	Intervention skill-building objective is clearly communicated to students.	Observation occurred 10 minutes into the class period; students were already working.
X			Intervention objectives are evident in student work samples.	
X			Interventionist delivers instruction consistent with program design.	Mr. Jackson was using scripted lesson plans aligned with the computer-based instruction and diagnostic assessments.
X			Intervention level matches student instructional level (measured at baseline).	
X			Repeated practice of objectives is aligned with measured skill deficits.	
X			Interventionist has necessary resources to deliver intervention as designed.	
X			Interventionist provides continuous constructive feedback to students.	Mr. Jackson continuously monitored the students and provided verbal praise and earned points for their participation and success.
X			Documented intervention time is consistent with RtI plan.	

and checklists for the implementation and documentation of the RtI process on campuses. Administrators should ensure that staff (particularly RtI team members) have a solid understanding of the district model and the data collection process and possess the necessary skills for analyzing the data. Documentation of related staff development activities for team members and other staff can be accomplished via a checklist that is kept with RtI data (discussed in chapter 3; see the sample staff training form on page 23).

Data collected to support documentation of the RtI process should include ongoing formative assessments of the process as well as an annual summative evaluation of progress over the year. If these data indicate that fidelity has been compromised, the team should formulate and implement an action plan. According to Burrus and Wallace (2008), conducting formative assessments of team processes is done in order to determine which aspects of the process are working and which need improvement. It is important that campus team problem solving be documented for the same purpose.

To generate strong documentation, the team must do the following:

✔ Review and revisit the district RtI guidelines on an ongoing basis throughout the year (documented on team meeting agendas; *hint:* include team member signatures to verify attendance).
✔ Ensure that team problem solving is consistent and that outcomes are analyzed (documented in team meeting notes).
✔ Use district-designed or district-adopted checklists, rubrics, and decision rules (done by simply having the district's guidelines for RtI implementation available at all team meetings).
✔ Determine how often and when formative reviews will be conducted (documented in team meeting minutes).
✔ Collect data at scheduled intervals (e.g., once or twice a week).
✔ Understand how to analyze and interpret the data (documented on the staff training form, page 23)
✔ Document the team meeting and formulate an action plan if needed for accountability.

One final piece of team process documentation is created by performing a summative assessment of the team problem-solving process, to explore whether that process results in progress for students who participated in multiple layers of interventions (i.e., an analysis of impact). Since the RtI process itself is not implemented solely to determine the need for special education evaluation, it is imperative that the team's data analysis document student movement between the RtI tiers. Essentially RtI is about moving a student within the tiers as data indicate changes in the level of intervention needed; therefore an effective team process results in the movement of some students within the tiers. Some students will need to be referred for special education evaluation, and the relevant data should be analyzed to determine campus and district qualification rates. It is recommended that the team annually document student movement by analyzing the records of students who received support. This information can be easily documented on an end-of-year review form (see page 74 for an example of a completed form).

RtI Team End-of-Year Review: Tier Summary Data

Campus: Wilson Elementary   Review Date: 6/6/11   Chair: Mr. Reynolds (Principal)

| | Tier 1 | Tier 2 | Tier 3 | Special Education Referrals | | Movement between Tiers | | | |
				Number Referred	Number Qualified	1 → 2	2 → 3	3 → 2	2 → 1
Kindergarten									
Reading	16	6	0	0	0	6	0	0	3
Math	2	0	0	0	0	0	0	0	0
Behavior	7	4	2	1	0	4	2	1	2
Grade 1									
Reading	28	17	10	5	1	17	10	8	6
Math	5	3	1	1	1	3	1	0	1
Behavior	12	2	2	0	0	2	2	0	0
Grade 2									
Reading	27	16	9	5	4	16	9	4	6
Math	11	7	6	3	3	7	6	1	1
Behavior	6	2	2	2	1	2	2	0	0
Grade 3									
Reading	17	14	6	6	4	14	6	2	5
Math	6	3	3	3	1	3	3	1	1
Behavior	3	1	1	0	0	1	1	0	0
Grade 4									
Reading	8	4	4	3	3	4	4	1	0
Math	9	6	2	1	1	6	2	1	4
Behavior	5	3	2	2	2	3	2	2	1
Grade 5									
Reading	9	5	4	2	1	5	4	3	2
Math	7	5	3	0	0	5	3	3	3
Behavior	3	1	0	0	0	1	0	0	0
Campus Totals	Tier 1	Tier 2	Tier 3	Number Referred	Number Qualified	1 → 2	2 → 3	3 → 2	2 → 1
Reading	105	62	33	21	13	62	33	18	22
Math	40	24	15	8	6	24	15	6	10
Behavior	36	13	9	5	3	13	9	3	3

Epilogue

Documentation is a vital aspect of the Response to Intervention process. It serves as the link between theory, practice, and outcomes for student success. When documenting, keep your team's focus on meeting the legal obligations of No Child Left Behind (2001), Section 504 of the 1973 Rehabilitation Act, and IDEA (2004) and on documenting the use of multiple sources of data (curriculum, instructional, student). Be vigilant in providing data—by thoroughly analyzing lesson plans, differentiation of content, and student work products—that demonstrate that all students on your campus have adequate access to instruction. Document your use of multiple assessments: formative, summative, diagnostic, progress monitoring, and outcomes. Your documentation of interventions must reflect an alignment with assessed student needs in foundational grade and content skills. Intertwined within all these areas is the documentation of fidelity.

Having district guidelines with published decision rules for your RtI problem-solving processes will ensure correct documentation of your RtI process. Additionally, make certain that staff receive professional development training in the areas of reading, math, adolescent literacy, assessment, and data-based decision making. District and campus administrators should serve as the instructional leaders by providing needed resources, coaching, and moral support for implementing the RtI process.

The parameters established in this book will assist in aligning your RtI framework with your district's process for helping struggling learners. The examples of forms and rubrics found here provide you with solid ideas for how to strengthen your documentation process. Remember: Do not focus on the forms, and do not overdocument. Keep your focus on the student.

And last but not least, here are some helpful tips for documentation:

12 Tips for Successful Documentation

1. The purpose of documentation is to develop instruction and intervention.
2. Never use documentation (or lack of it) for delaying a special education evaluation when there is strong evidence of a suspected disability.
3. Focus documentation on converging multiple sources of data. (Use formative assessments to focus instruction on state standards; diagnostics to pinpoint student problems; progress monitoring to determine response to intervention; and outcomes assessment to analyze adequate yearly progress.)
4. Keep it simple. Use naturally occurring data to drive RtI problem solving.
5. Consistency is key.
6. Create rubrics for teams to follow.
7. Train staff on data collection and data analysis.
8. Develop user-friendly forms. (*Hint:* Use the forms in this book as templates.)
9. Keep problem solving within the domain of general education.
10. Tie your documentation to evidence-based practices.
11. Do not forget the importance of documenting academic engagement time.
12. Fidelity, fidelity, fidelity. *Remember:* If it isn't documented, then it did not happen!

School District Guidance Document: Response to Intervention

Mission Statement

The mission of XYZ School District is to assist all students in achieving grade-level success. XYZ School District will provide relevant, challenging, and diverse educational opportunities for all students in a safe environment, so that they will be lifelong learners who realize their potential to become successful, collaborative citizens.

Contents

Laws Supporting Response to Intervention (RtI)

Both the No Child Left Behind Act (NCLB 2001) and the Individuals with Disabilities Education Improvement Act (IDEA 2004) focus on the quality of instruction that students receive in the general education setting. NCLB and IDEA require the use of research-based instruction and interventions. RtI focuses on effective academic and behavioral programs that result in improved student performance.

Using data-based interventions and interventions based on scientific research to determine eligibility for learning disabilities is stressed in IDEA 2004. With an RtI approach, general education teachers assume increased responsibility for delivering high-quality instruction to early-identified struggling students. The diverse needs of these students must be addressed through a tiered problem-solving system of timely interventions that increase in intensity and duration. RtI promotes the unity of general education and special education to create a seamless system.

Defining "Response to Intervention"

Response to Intervention, or RtI, is the practice of meeting the academic and behavioral needs of all students through a problem-solving process with three key elements:

- High-quality instruction and research-based tiered interventions aligned with individual student need
- Frequent monitoring of student progress to enable results-based academic and/or behavioral decisions
- Use of student response data in making important educational decisions (such as those regarding placement, intervention, curriculum, and instructional goals and methodologies)

The instructional approaches within the general education setting should result in academic and/or behavioral progress for the majority of the students (80%). The primary focus of RtI is early intervention to prevent long-term academic failure. Struggling students are identified using data-based progress monitoring and are provided intensive instruction. The use of a scientifically validated curriculum, as well as instructional methods expected in an RtI model, leads to school improvement. Support services require collaboration among campus personnel such as counselors, interventionists, special education teachers, and dyslexia teachers.

The Major Components of RtI

Data-based decision making—Critical educational decisions are based on assessment results. Data are carefully analyzed to determine why academic or behavioral problems exist.

Universal screening—Universal screenings are assessments administered to all students to determine as early as possible which students are at risk of not meeting academic benchmarks. These screenings are administered three times per year in order to meet early intervention needs of all students.

Tiered model of delivery—The RtI process incorporates a tiered model of delivery of instruction. The tiers reflect increasing intensification of interventions to meet the individual needs of students.

Progress monitoring—The monitoring of student progress is a research-based practice that produces data about student growth over time. Progress monitoring is used to determine the effectiveness of instruction and/or interventions.

Fidelity of implementation—Fidelity of implementation is achieved when the delivery of instruction, assessments, and progress monitoring is carried out as it was designed to be.

Characteristics of RtI

- RtI meets the goals of the No Child Left Behind Act by helping with early identification of struggling learners and by providing immediate intervention using scientific, research-based instruction and teaching methods in order to improve educational outcomes.
- RtI is a preventive approach used to intervene early when students show signs of not meeting grade-level standards.
- RtI generates high-quality instruction and interventions matched to student needs.
- RTI uses the student's learning rate and level of performance to make educational decisions.
- RtI can be used to make referral decisions for students who do not respond to intensive intervention (Tier 3) in the general education setting.
- RtI provides data that can be used in the identification of students with specific learning disabilities, as opposed to the traditional discrepancy model used to determine eligibility for special education services.
- RtI meets the educational needs of all students by providing direct, focused instruction to address specific academic and/or behavioral needs.

The Three Tiers of RtI

Tier 1

Tier 1 is the foundation of the RtI instructional model. In this tier, all students receive high-quality, research-based instruction in the general education setting. Teachers deliver high-quality core class instruction that is aligned with state standards and in which 80% or more of the students are successful.

Students in grades K–9 will be screened three times a year with valid and reliable reading, mathematics, and behavioral assessments to determine areas where intervention is needed. Students will be identified as "at risk" and assigned a case facilitator in Tier 1 if they score below the district cut score on the universal screening and demonstrate a lack of grade-level success through a review of multiple data sources. Teachers will differentiate instruction in grade-level classes for 6 weeks and will monitor the progress of all students via documentation of universal screening and individual student results on state assessments, curriculum-based assessments, district benchmark assessments, daily assignments, and teacher-made assessments. All interventions must be explicit and documented. The classroom teacher and the case facilitator will assess the progress of identified Tier 1 students in the general education setting every 2 weeks during this period to determine whether the intervention is working.

Tier 2

The RtI campus team may increase support to Tier 2 for students who are not making progress at Tier 1, typically about 10–15% of all students. Students are identified for individualized small-group instruction delivered by teachers and interventionists, in addition to core class instruction. This intensified level of intervention includes research-based programs, strategies, and procedures designed to supplement and enhance Tier 1 activities, including hands-on manipulatives and computer-assisted learning.

Students who are performing at Tier 2 levels will receive strategic instruction as follows:

Grades	Tier 2 intervention delivery
K–6	Minimum of 30 minutes, 3 times a week, for two 6-week periods
7 and 8	Homogeneous grouping of students for 45 minutes, 3 times a week, for two 6-week periods
9 and 10	Homogeneous grouping of students for 130 minutes weekly, for two 6-week periods

Tier 3

Students who have not responded adequately to interventions in Tiers 1 and 2 and are performing significantly below grade level will move to Tier 3 and receive intensified, comprehensive intervention in addition to their grade-level curriculum. Tier 3 typically addresses the needs of approximately 5–10% of all students.

Grades	Tier 3 intervention delivery
K–6	Minimum of 45 minutes, 5 times a week, for 6 weeks
7 and 8	60 minutes daily for 6 weeks
9 and 10	60 minutes daily for 6 weeks

Reading and Mathematics

The measures to be used for universal screening in reading and mathematics are listed below.

Grades K–1

Reading—Istation (assessment component)

Mathematics—Early Numeracy (CBM)
- Oral counting
- Number identification
- Quantity discrimination
- Missing number

Grades 2–10

Reading—Istation (assessment component)
- Phonemic awareness
- Phonics
- Vocabulary
- Fluency
- Comprehension
- Historical data

Mathematics—CBM
- Mathematics concepts and applications
- Historical data

District Nonnegotiables

- The responsibility of the RtI team within each school will be the school's administrator or the administrator's designee.
- Universal screenings will be administered three times a year (fall, winter, and spring) to all students in grades K–10, according to the district schedule.
- Interventions will be implemented with fidelity.
- Weekly meetings will be held with documented meeting minutes.
- Documentation will be collected by teachers, case facilitators, and interventionists and will be reviewed at regularly scheduled meetings focusing on assessment, interventions, and fidelity.
- Student intervention plans will be reviewed every 6 weeks.
- Data will be used to make any necessary additions or other changes to student intervention plans.
- Student privacy is of the highest priority with the RtI team, requiring that all team members take an oath of confidentiality.

District RtI Decision-Making Guide

Tier 1

Reading universal screening: fall, winter, spring
     Istation for grades K–4 (Eng), district-provided
     Maze passages for grades 5–9
     Istation (Eng/*Sp) and Tejas LEE for grades K–2 (Sp)
        (*Use Istation Spanish version if students are identified as at risk in both Istation English and Tejas LEE)
     TALA for grades 7–8

Math universal screening: fall, winter, spring
     District-provided for grades K–9

- Cut score = 20th percentile.
- Principal/administrator chairs a meeting with the campus RtI team. Data are analyzed to identify data trends for students whose scores fall below the cut score. RtI team consults with teachers regarding curriculum and instructional practices.
- Teachers implement core curriculum and interventions for 6 weeks. Teacher administers assessment once a week and provides progress-monitoring data to the RtI team. The team reviews classroom and progress-monitoring data with the case facilitator and analyzes the progress of designated Tier 1 at-risk students.
    - → *Decision point: week 6.* Identify students who continue to score below the cut score on week 6 screening and demonstrate a lack of progress. Schedule RtI meetings to discuss student move to Tier 2.

Tier 2
Strategic interventions: 12 weeks

- Use research-based fluency average learning rates for goal setting (Fuchs et al. 2006).
- Establish baseline data-point scores and develop aimline (goal).
- Select appropriate intervention, to be delivered in a 30-minute session, 3 times per week.
- Discuss intervention effectiveness and problem-solve as needed (use RtI standard protocol).
- Assign intervention support and assessment support.
- Begin intervention. Group size is 5–6 (elementary) and 6–8 (intermediate and up).
- Administer progress-monitoring assessment 2 times per week.
  - ➜ *Decision point: week 6.* Use a three-data-point decision rule to monitor progress, and problem-solve if the intervention needs to be altered.
- Continue intervention.
  - ➜ *Decision point: week 12.* Reconvene the RtI team and analyze the data collected. If the learning rate has increased, continue the intervention. If not, change the intervention and monitor progress; *or* if the learning rate falls significantly below established norms, begin Tier 3 interventions.

Tier 3
Intensive interventions: 6 weeks

- Increase intensity of intervention to a 60-minute session, 5 times a week.
- Discuss intervention effectiveness and problem-solve as needed (use RtI standard protocol).
- Continue intervention support and assessment support.
- Begin intervention. Group size is 3 (all grade levels).
- Increase progress monitoring to 3 times per week.
  - ➜ *Decision point: week 6.* If the learning rate has increased, continue the intervention or exit to Tier 2. If the learning rate has not increased, refer the student for Section 504 or special education evaluation.

Note: It is suggested that districts insert flowcharts to provide a visual representation of the RtI process here. Information on developing academic and behavioral flowcharts can be found in *The Response to Intervention Handbook: Moving from Theory to Practice* (Ogonosky 2009), *Response to Intervention in Secondary Schools* (Ogonosky 2010), and *RTI—Three Tiers of Behavior* (Ogonosky and Mintsioulis 2010).

Frequently Asked Questions

What is the purpose of the RtI team?

Each campus will have a team that implements an RtI approach, according to the process outlined in the model adopted by the district. The purpose of the team is to make data-based decisions regarding students who are experiencing difficulties in academic and/or behavioral domains. The team will develop an intervention plan to promote improvements in the student's academic performance and/or classroom behavior and will provide the teacher with support to implement the interventions. Teachers will be provided the support and resources they need to implement the interventions at each of the three RtI tiers.

Who is on the RtI team?

Each campus will have a core team (5 or 6 members) that will meet regularly at specified dates and times. The team is accountable for most of the RtI process and is multidisciplinary, including an administrator, a counselor, a diagnostician, a classroom teacher or teachers, an interventionist, and parents.

Campus administrator—Participation by an administrator is key to the RtI team's effectiveness. The administrator's responsibilities include the following:
- Scheduling the team meeting's time and location
- Maintaining communication between the team members, the principal, and administrative staff
- Recruiting new members
- Maintaining documentation of the team process
- Scheduling and attending additional meetings when deemed necessary
- Ensuring that the RtI team process is monitored and evaluated for effectiveness
- Participating in a district-wide RtI planning committee

Case facilitator—Each identified student must have an assigned case facilitator. Most team members will function in this role at some time on a rotating basis. The case facilitator is responsible for the following:
- Aiding teachers and staff in communicating with the assigned data collector
- Examining existing data, such as grades, attendance records, cumulative folder, and discipline folder
- Consulting with the school nurse and other staff for feedback
- Participating in meetings with parents, if scheduled
- Monitoring the intervention process as indicated in the RtI plan

Data collector—The data collector gathers information, organizes the presentation of data, manages data reports on interventions, and plots student progress.
All students identified within the RtI process need to be monitored so that the

intervention outcome can be measured. (This monitoring is the responsibility of the assigned case facilitator.) The data collector is responsible for the following:

- Gathering and comparing measurable data to determine the outcome of the RtI plan
- Creating a report for the campus RtI team, highlighting the effectiveness of the instructional support plan for individual students, as well as the overall process

Record keeper—This team member is responsible for scripting and documenting the meetings.

Timekeeper (optional) —To keep the group on task and the meetings within their allotted amount of time, one team member may serve as a timekeeper, using a timer to structure the pace of the meeting.

Who conducts the campus-wide screening process?

The campus RtI team is responsible for overseeing the universal screening process. Universal screenings will be conducted on every student. The classroom teacher or other school personnel conduct the screenings and report the results to the campus RtI team. Careful documentation of screening results is important for accurate identification of students' needs.

If the results of universal screening suggest that an individual student is performing below standards, then interventions by the classroom teacher need to be developed and implemented at Tier 1. District-approved interventions are used to prevent students from failing to meet academic and/or behavioral expectations and thus requiring more intensive interventions. The goal of district-approved interventions is to proactively teach and support desired academic and social behavior for all students. Confidentiality must be safeguarded, although district-approved screening records should be accessible to teachers and staff who work with a student. *Note: Universal screening is not considered to be an individual evaluation and therefore does not require prior parental notice or consent.*

What happens during Tier 1?

- All students are provided high-quality core instructional and behavioral supports in the general education setting.
- Universal screenings of mathematics and reading are administered to all students by a team of school personnel and/or the classroom teacher to determine each student's level of proficiency.
- A team approach is used to analyze and screen data to identify any problem areas in the curriculum, instruction, the environment, or learners.
- Using the problem-solving model, the RtI team defines the problem in concrete, measurable terms.
- Differentiated instruction is used within the classroom, and student response to the instruction is monitored.
- Adjustments in instructional strategies for all students in the classroom are reflected through whole-group and small-group differentiated instruction.
- Identified students are provided interventions based on data from ongoing assessments.

- Identified students receive interventions usually in small, teacher-led flexible groups. The intervention occurs during the regular school day in the general education classroom with a review of student progress every 2 weeks.
- The intervention schedule is based on how frequently the teacher needs to meet with and provide direct instruction to each group per week (e.g., *group meets daily, group meets 3 times per week*) and the number of minutes per meeting time (e.g., *10 minutes, 20 minutes*).
- A progress monitoring tool is used to track students' response to intervention, and a minimum of 3 data points are collected within 6 weeks.
- Campus administrators monitor the fidelity and integrity of classroom instruction and interventions.
- Interventions and progress are documented in the student's instructional support plan, which is kept in the student's RtI folder.

What critical areas need to be addressed in Tier 1 classroom interventions?

The Individuals with Disabilities Improvement Act of 2004 (IDEA) and the No Child Left Behind Act of 2001 (NCLB) advocate the use of interventions and instruction based on scientific research. Both acts require effective reading and mathematics instruction that results in improved student performance and a reduction in the number of students needing special education services. Essential components for reading are phonemic awareness, vocabulary development, reading comprehension, phonics instruction, and fluency, and those for mathematics are mathematics calculation and problem solving.

What happens during Tier 2?

- Tier 2 instruction/interventions are delivered inside the classroom or in a pull-out setting outside the classroom to students who are not achieving state and grade-level standards through core instruction and district-approved Tier 1 interventions.
- Identified students are provided with research-based interventions based on data from ongoing assessments.
- Small, flexible, teacher-led instructional groups are formed, based on student data and observations.
- Students with similar instructional needs are grouped together, limiting the size of the group according to the intensity of instruction needed.
- Identified students in grades K–10 receive interventions in small groups during the regular school day for two 6-week periods.
- Academic instructional time is increased. How often and how long the teacher meets with each small group varies, depending on student needs.
- Campus administrators monitor the fidelity and integrity of classroom instruction and interventions.
- The CBM data are used to assess student response.
- Instruction is adjusted, based on each student's response to the provided intervention.
- Interventions and student progress are documented in the Tier 2 intervention plan.
- A progress-monitoring tool is used to identify which students continue to need assistance and to determine the specific kinds of skill deficits that must be addressed.

- The collaborative RtI team analyzes assessment data, determines the progress that has or has not been made, develops individualized interventions, monitors interventions, and identifies students who need further support provided at Tier 3 or with special education.

What happens during Tier 3?

- Individualized instruction is provided in addition to core instruction in the general education classroom.
- Multiple interventions and services are delivered by specially trained staff.
- The student-teacher ratio is reduced.
- The intensity and frequency of support services are adjusted as students achieve targeted skills. Students continue to move fluidly between and among the tiers.
- Instructional time is increased.
- Student progress is tracked weekly, using progress-monitoring tools to determine intervention effectiveness and the students' response to the intervention(s).
- Campus administrators monitor the fidelity and integrity of classroom instruction and interventions.

NOTE: The school district may insert here a list of the most frequently asked questions that district-level staff receive regarding RtI. When compiling these questions, you may wish to refer to the book RTI-FAQs *(Ogonosky 2010).*

Common RtI Abbreviations and Terms

CBM   curriculum-based measurement
IDEA   Individuals with Disabilities Education Improvement Act of 2004
IEP   individualized education plan
LD   learning disability
NCLB   No Child Left Behind Act of 2001
PBS   positive behavior support
RtI   Response to Intervention

academic engagement time   The amount of time a student is actively participating in instruction (excluding transition times).
aimline   A visual representation (line) on a progress-monitoring graph that connects the baseline data point to the outcome goal.
baseline data point   An initial score that indicates a student's skill level before intervention; the starting point in curriculum-based measurement of the student's response to the intervention.
behavior action plan   A plan designed by the campus RtI team to teach appropriate behavior strategies and responses to students.
benchmark   An assessment of group performance against a standard at defined points in time to measure progress toward meeting the standard.
case facilitator   An RtI committee member assigned to consult with staff regarding a student's needs and interventions.
clinical utility   The capacity to make a decision possible, based upon the data presented.
common assessments   Assessments created by a team of educators for identifying students who need additional time and support and for designing instructional strategies to promote skill acquisition.
core curriculum   Instructional content that specifies skills aligned with grade-level state standards that must be addressed.
curriculum-based measurement (CBM)   Any set of assessment procedures that uses direct observation and recording of a student's performance in a local curriculum to gather information for making instructional decisions.
cut score   Within RtI, a preset score against which assessment results can be compared to help RtI teams identify struggling learners.
data-based decision making   The process of analyzing assessment data to determine why a student's academic or behavioral problem exists and then deciding on a research-based strategy to address the specific problem.
differentiation of instruction   An approach to teaching and learning in which students have multiple options for taking in information, making sense of ideas, and demonstrating their understanding; requires teachers to be flexible in adjusting their methods and the curriculum to suit students, rather than expecting students to modify themselves for the curriculum.

fidelity   The degree to which something is carried out as designed, intended, and planned.

fluency   An acceptable level of mastery of a skill.

formative assessment   A dynamic aspect of the instructional process that provides information for making timely adjustments to enhance learning; considered integral to developing the delivery of instruction by evaluating the delivery and relevance of the curriculum.

functional behavioral assessment   A collection of information about events that predict and maintain a student's problem behavior; used to construct a behavior action plan.

instructional level   A level of the curriculum that is challenging to a student, but not so challenging that the student is frustrated.

intervention   Any process that is intended to increase learning or modify a student's behavior.

lack of progress   A student's failure to demonstrate expected learning rates relative to the baseline data point after an RtI intervention plan has been implemented with fidelity.

learning rate   The pace of a student's skill acquisition; one of the elements used for making decisions in RtI.

multigate system   A system that uses multiple steps and indicators for identifying students who are at risk for emotional and behavior problems.

norm-referenced assessment   A measure of performance in terms of an individual's standing in some known group, such as all of a district's students at a particular grade level.

outcome goal   The targeted goal of an intervention plan.

probes   In terms of progress monitoring and curriculum-based measurement, refers to brief repeated assessments of an academic skill.

progress monitoring   Frequent measurement of student progress in a brief, repeatable, reliable, and scientifically valid way; usually performed at predetermined intervals to allow for timely modification of instructional design to suit the student's needs.

research-based strategies   Instructional designs and recommendations that have been demonstrated through formal scientific research to improve learning.

RtI model   A conception of the process known as Response to Intervention for delivering research-based instruction and interventions to facilitate student learning.

RtI standard protocol   A method of problem solving that provides structure for choosing appropriate standard interventions to address the most common student weaknesses.

summative assessment   Assessment that is used to give a grade to a student; a measure of cumulative student learning, such as an end-of-semester exam or a state-mandated test.

three-data-point decision rule   A decision-making rule within the RtI problem-solving process that analyzes three consecutive progress-monitoring data points against the expected goal (must have a minimum of nine data points).

universal screening   A type of assessment administered to all students to determine, as early as possible, which students are likely to experience difficulty learning, due to a lack of foundational skills. Universal screenings are used as predictors of success within a grade level and are administered three times per year in order to meet early-intervention needs of all students.

Appendix B
Multiple Intelligence and Learning Style Inventories: Resources for Your RtI Toolkit

The following list contains sources for the multiple intelligence and learning style inventories that I have found most helpful when working with RtI teams. At these websites you'll also find useful general information about multiple intelligences and learning styles.

What's Your Learning Style? (K–12)
www.ldpride.net/learning-style-test.html

Free VAK Learning Styles Test (K–12)
www.businessballs.com/vaklearningstylestest.htm

Assessment: Find Your Strengths! (grade 3 and above)
http://literacyworks.org/mi/assessment/findyourstrengths.html

A Multiple Intelligences Primer (secondary students)
www.personal.psu.edu/staff/b/x/bxb11/MI/index.htm

What's Your Learning Style?
http://agelesslearner.com/assess/learningstyle.html

Index of Learning Styles Questionnaire
www.engr.ncsu.edu/learningstyles/ilsweb.html

How Many Ways Are *You* Smart?
www.lauracandler.com/strategies/CL/misurvey.pdf

Appendix C

Tier 1 Responsibilities of the Case Facilitator

Essential Case Facilitator Responsibilities for Consultation in Tier 1

1. **After universal screening has been administered,** the campus RtI team (of which the case facilitator is a member) completes the following tasks:
   a. Reviews the universal screening data on all students and analyze trends.
   b. Makes team-member assignments for each of the students to be supported.
      i. Assigns the staff member (an administrator) who will be responsible for checking fidelity.
      ii. Assigns the staff member (other than the case facilitator) who will be responsible for student observation.
   c. Schedules and documents a teacher consultation to discuss the following (this consultation occurs no later than 1 week after the initial team meeting):
      i. Concerns about the student
      ii. Tier 1 strategies to address these concerns
      iii. How to accomplish the reading, math, or behavior documentation
      iv. Program-monitoring technique to be used

2. **Within a week after the teacher consultation,** the case facilitator meets with the student's teacher (or teachers) to do the following:
   a. Determine whether the teacher has begun implementing a Tier 1 strategy. If not, the case facilitator and the teacher problem-solve together to find out why not and what support the teacher needs (e.g., the facilitator assists the teacher with finding proper resources and/or informs the RtI team of the teacher's need for support).
   b. Determine whether the teacher has any questions regarding the strategies
   c. Determine whether the teacher needs any additional resources to implement the strategies
   d. Determine whether the teacher is still satisfied with the strategies designed. If not, the case facilitator and the teacher problem-solve together to minimally modify strategy and/or the case facilitator informs the RtI team.
   e. Update documentation to include additional information collected since the previous consultation.

3. The case facilitator checks with the student's teacher (or teachers) approximately **every 2 weeks for the duration of the intervention** and performs the following tasks:
   a. Determines whether the strategy and the program monitoring are being implemented as designed.
   b. Determines whether the teacher is maintaining the appropriate documentation
   c. Documents the conversations and any additional information provided by teacher
   d. Reports back to the RtI team regarding student progress.

RtI Team Documentation Checklist

Campus: _____ Case Facilitator: _____

Student: _____ Grade: _____ Teacher(s): _____

Tier 1 Documentation (ongoing and completed every 6 weeks)

_____ Review of universal screening trends - Dates:_____, _____, _____

_____ Review of lesson plans in area of concern

_____ Review of student work samples

_____ Review of case facilitator consultation documentation

_____ Review of classroom observations focusing on curriculum, instruction, environment, and learner

_____ Review of fidelity checks

_____ Review of 4 sources of assessment (screening, diagnostics, progress monitoring, outcomes)

Note: All sources of documentation are attached to the team meeting form used by the district.

Tier 2 Documentation (weekly progress monitoring and completed every 6 weeks)

_____ Review of intervention design

_____ Review of intervention alignment with diagnostic and progress-monitoring data

_____ Review of student growth (Tier 1 grade level; include all formative assessments and student work samples)

_____ Review of student growth (Tier 2 instructional level, measured by diagnostics and progress monitoring)

_____ Fidelity checks on Tier 2 intervention

_____ Team decisions regarding analysis of multiple sources of data, intervention status, and student support (change in tiers, etc.).

*Note: These data are **collected** with the ongoing Tier 1 data collection.*

Tier 3 Documentation (intensified weekly progress monitoring and completed in 4–6 weeks)

_____ Review of intervention design

_____ Review of intervention alignment with diagnostic and progress-monitoring data

_____ Review of student growth (Tier 1 grade level); include all formative assessments and student work samples)

_____ Review of student growth (Tier 3 instructional level measured by diagnostics and progress monitoring)

_____ Fidelity checks on Tier 3 intervention

_____ Team decisions regarding analysis of multiple sources of data, intervention status, and student support (change in tiers, etc.).

Note: These data are collected with the ongoing Tier 1 data collection.

Referral for Section 504 or Special Education Evaluation

_____ Completion of district forms (include all RtI problem-solving information) - Date: _____

RtI Team Documentation: Staff Training

TIER 1 *High-quality instructional and behavioral supports are provided for all students within general education.*

	Training Date	Coaching Date	Teacher Implementation Date
Universal screening	_____	_____	_____
Diagnostics	_____	_____	_____
Progress monitoring	_____	_____	_____

Description of Content
- Collection and sharing of benchmark data among teachers, principals, district staff, and parents (data are collected in fall, winter, and spring)
- Specific, objective measures of problem areas, not anecdotal information or opinions

TIER 2 *Students whose performance and rate of progress lag behind those of peers in their classroom, school, or district receive more-specialized prevention or remediation within general education.*

	Training Date	Coaching Date	Teacher Implementation Date
Baseline data collection	_____	_____	_____
Diagnostics	_____	_____	_____
Progress monitoring	_____	_____	_____
Written plan of accountability	_____	_____	_____
Comparison of pre- and post- intervention data	_____	_____	_____

Description of Content
- Curriculum-based measurement (CBM) to determine whether the problem area is an issue with the student or the core curriculum
- Which interventions will be tried that are different? Who will deliver them? When? Where? For how long?
- Frequent collection of a variety of data for examining student performance over time and evaluating interventions, in order to make data-based decisions
- Data-based decision making for intervention effectiveness

TIER 3 *Tier 3 includes all the elements of Tier 2. The difference between Tier 2 and Tier 3 is the frequency and group size of the intervention treatment.*

	Training Date
Increased intensity of interventions	_____

Description of Content
- The most intensive phase of RtI
- Fidelity of intervention ensured by documentation
- Referral for multidisciplinary assessment for special education if progress monitoring does not establish improvement after intervention phase is implemented

Source: Adapted from Ogonosky, Booth, and Cheramie 2006.

RtI Team Documentation: Tier 1 Lesson Plan Review

Teacher: _____ Content Area: _____ Grade: _____ Date of Review: _____

Lesson Plan Element	Excellent (4 points)	Accomplished (3 points)	Satisfactory (2 points)	Beginning (1 point)	Score
Alignment with state standards	Lesson supports core curriculum, aligned to state standards. Benchmarks are stated and appropriately used to guide lesson plan development.	Lesson provides connections to core curriculum, referenced to state standards. Benchmarks are stated and connected to lesson plan development.	Lesson appears to relate to core curriculum and state standards, but alignment is not explicit. Benchmarks are stated but not explicitly connected to lesson plan development.	Lesson does not provide connection to core curriculum or state standards. Benchmark information is absent.	
Instructional goals and objectives	Goals and objectives are stated clearly and aligned to standards incorporating concepts, principles, and cognitive skills within the area of study. Lesson plan provides a list of student outcomes at end of lesson. Learners can determine what they should know and be able to do as a result of instruction.	Goals and objectives are stated. Objectives are listed and reference standards. Learners are able to determine what they should know and be able to do as a result of instruction.	Goals and objectives are provided but are not clear and might not be realistic, given the lesson content. Objectives do not sufficiently address benchmarks.	Objectives are not listed, are unclear, and do not align with state standards or benchmarks.	
Instructional strategies	Differentiated instructional strategies are stated clearly and aligned with evidence-based practices. Lesson procedures are complete, deep, and flexible. Lesson offers extensions for higher-level learning, and adaptations are evident for students with special needs. Plan identifies potential barriers to lesson and offers alternative instructional strategies.	Most strategies are appropriate to learning and are evidence based. Lesson procedures are complete but lack depth in details for adapting lesson for higher-level learning. Plan is not complete in adaptations for students with special needs. Lesson is not clear on addressing potential barrier, nor does it offer alternative strategies.	Some strategies are appropriated and have evidence-based support. Procedure lacks depth and does not offer strategies for adaptations to students with higher-order learning or special needs. Teacher may need to seek out resources for completion of lesson.	Instructional strategies are missing or are not appropriate to lesson content. Lesson appears incomplete. Teacher role is not clearly defined. Teacher will need to invest significant time and effort in order to implement lesson.	
Learning tasks	Tasks are listed that are aligned with goals and objectives of lesson. Task concepts are engaging in reasoning, reflection, analysis, and synthesis of learning and evaluation of information. Students create their own product/process. Tasks build on previously learned information and require student to build on that knowledge. Authentic learning experiences are provided.	Most tasks are aligned with goal and objectives. Most tasks are engaging in reasoning, reflection, analysis and synthesis of learning and evaluation of information. Tasks require students to investigate and create their own product/process. Most tasks build on previously learned information.	Tasks are somewhat aligned to goals and objectives. The tasks engage students in the application of previously learned material using multiple representations, but students are not required to make connections among them.	Tasks listed are tangentially related to goals and objectives. Tasks require only limited practice. Student task completion relies on recall and identification only of previously learned information. The structure of the tasks listed does not encourage intrinsic motivation.	

Lesson Plan Element	Excellent (4 points)	Accomplished (3 points)	Satisfactory (2 points)	Beginning (1 point)	Score
Resources	All needed materials are listed. Necessary supplies are readily accessible through technology or teacher resources center.	Plan has a materials list but is missing some details. Most supplies appear to be available through technology or teacher resource center.	Plan has a materials list, but important details may be missing such as quantity and type of materials. Tangential connections to technology resources are listed.	Items essential for plan implementation are not evident or listed. Details are omitted. and little information is available regarding access to technology or teacher resources.	
Assessment	Assessments are aligned with benchmarks and lesson objectives. Strategies are described in detail for data collection. Rubrics for scoring are included. Design of assessment is for progress monitoring, feedback, and differentiation of content.	Some assessments are aligned with benchmarks and lesson objectives. Design of assessment is diagnostic and evaluative, with some reference to progress monitoring.	Assessments appear related to benchmarks and lesson objectives. Assessment information is vague and may or may not be designed to drive instruction.	There is no evidence of assessment connected to benchmarks or lesson objectives. Reference to assessment relies solely on paper-and-pencil tasks or outcomes.	
Use of technology	Plan provides information for access to real-world situations through video, audio, graphics. Multisensory applications are represented and provide multiple opportunities for skill building. Selection and application of technology are appropriate to learning environment and outcomes.	Plan provides for use of technology to enable students to be meaningfully involved in real-world applications using video, audio, graphics. Lesson's use of technology encourages student involvement in use of technology and is appropriate.	Plan lists technology but is not focused and does not drive student involvement to affect learning outcomes.	Plan lists technology that is not appropriate to learning outcomes or environment. The technology treats students as passive recipients of information and is not clearly designed.	
Total points per column					

Scoring Rubric for RtI Team Documentation of Tier 1 Lesson Plan Review

27–28 points: Excellent   25–26 points: Accomplished   23–24 points: Satisfactory   Below 23 points: Beginning

Note: If score is below 23, team will problem-solve to determine which supports are needed and how the lesson plan needs to be redesigned to align at-risk learners with access to curriculum and instruction.

RtI Team Documentation: Tier 1 Instructional Strategies for Increasing Academic Engagement Time

Teacher/Content Area: _____   Student: _____   Date: _____

Key Points	Salient Features	Consistency of Implementation	Fidelity Check
High-quality, research-based activities	Yes No Are aligned with state curriculum standards/content objectives. Yes No Are rigorous and relevant to content designed for high student interest and multisensory involvement. Yes No Provide students with choice of activity. Yes No Assess student age, interests, needs, learning styles, and developmental level when designing activity. Yes No Use a variety of activities in order to avoid practice effects and saturation, which can inhibit on-task engagement.	Attendance Work Samples Classroom Observations Notes:	Fidelity Check Classroom Observations Lesson Plan Review Notes:
Positive outcomes for students	Yes No Students take ownership in their learning. Yes No Student engagement increases when students are presented with activities based on their interest and ability level. Yes No Allowing for choice of product increases student motivation. Yes No Ability to build foundational skills increases when activity is individualized for students.	Attendance Work Samples Classroom Observations Notes:	Fidelity Check Classroom Observations Lesson Plan Review Notes:
Teacher planning	Yes No Review curriculum strands based on state expectations. Yes No Determine which materials and resources are necessary. Yes No Align activity with direct instruction embedded in lesson plans. Yes No Determine product assessment tool (e.g., rubrics) and evaluation methods. Yes No Plan for sharing with grade/content teachers.	Attendance Work Samples Classroom Observations Notes:	Fidelity Check Classroom Observations Lesson Plan Review Notes:

We assure that the above-noted intervention(s) were conducted as disclosed.

_____   _____   _____
Principal/ RtI Team Chair   Classroom Teacher/Service Provider   Case Facilitator

RtI Classroom Observations

Student:_____ Grade:_____ Date of Observation: _____

Teacher: _____ Campus: _____

Observer: _____ Time of Day: From _____ to _____

Teacher-Student Ratio:_____ Instructional Level of Lesson:_____

Time on Task: *(Circle* **on task [+]** *or* **off task [−]** *at 10-second intervals.)*

+ −	+ −	+ −	+ −	+ −	+ −	+ −	+ −	+ −	+ −	+ −	+ −	+ −	+ −	+ −

Class/Subject Observed: *(Observation should be in the area of suspected disability.)*

○ English/LA	○ Reading	○ History/Social Studies	○ Science
○ Math	○ Specials	○ Other:	○ Other:

Student-Teacher Ratio during Observation Period:

Students:	○ Fewer than 10	○ 10–15	○ 16–20	○ More than 20

Classroom Arrangement:

○ Rows of desks	○ Grouped desks	○ Tables	○ Centers	○ Other:

Classroom Interaction with Teacher:	Yes	No	Not Observed	Comments:
Demanded teacher attention	○	○	○	
Was attentive to instruction/instructor	○	○	○	
Had excessive concern with achievement	○	○	○	
Participated in class discussion	○	○	○	
Responded appropriately to: Praise	○	○	○	
Correction	○	○	○	
Required firm discipline	○	○	○	
Was out of seat without permission	○	○	○	

Work Behavior:				
Began tasks promptly	○	○	○	
Had short attention span	○	○	○	
Was easily distracted	○	○	○	
Appeared prepared and organized for activity	○	○	○	
Follows oral instruction	○	○	○	
Follows written instruction	○	○	○	
Works effectively in: Small group	○	○	○	
Large group	○	○	○	
Alone	○	○	○	
Appears to work to limit of ability	○	○	○	

Classroom Interaction with Peers:				
Interacts with peers appropriately	○	○	○	
Disturbed others: Frequently	○	○	○	
Occasionally	○	○	○	
Not at any time	○	○	○	

Comments: _____

_____

_____

Signature of Observer _____ Position _____

RtI Team Documentation: Tier 1 Problem Solving

(Complete this form after universal screenings have been administered.)

Campus: _____Date: _____Date of Screening:_____

Grade: _____   Area: Reading _____Math _____   Cut Score: _____

TEAM DATA ANALYSIS

PLAN OF ACTION FOR TIER 1 CURRICULUM AND INSTRUCTION

MEMBERS IN ATTENDANCE

_____   _____

_____   _____

_____   _____

_____   _____

RtI Documentation: Problem Specification Checklist for Tier 1 Case Facilitator Initial Consultation

(Limit to 2 primary areas.)

Student:_____ Teacher: _____

Case Facilitator:_____ Return by: _____

Academic Readiness
_____Recall of personal information
_____Shape recognition
_____Color recognition
_____1:1 correspondence
_____Number identification
_____Uppercase letter identification
_____Lowercase letter identification
_____Counting
_____Recitation of alphabet
_____Other areas: _____

Language
_____Expressive language
_____Receptive language

Reading
_____Pre-literacy skills
      Specify:

_____Sight words
_____Fluency: (accuracy and quickness)
_____Vocabulary development
_____Comprehension

Math
_____Quantity
_____Number recognition
_____Number concepts
_____Calculation accuracy
_____Applications
_____Word problems
_____Measurement
_____Pre-algebra concepts
_____Math vocabulary

Writing
_____Fine motor or handwriting
_____Conventions (punctuation, capitalization)
_____Language (sentence structure, grammar, vocabulary)
_____Construction of story (prose, action, sequence, theme)
_____Fluency
_____Spelling

Behavior
Description (type, frequency, duration, setting):

_____
_____
_____
_____
_____

Please complete and return to the RtI team after initial teacher consultation.

RtI Documentation: Tier 1 Case Facilitator Follow-up

Student:_____Teacher: _____

Case Facilitator:_____Initial Contact Date: _____

Week_____Tier _____
Are the interventions being implemented as designed?   Y / N
If not, why not?_____

_____

Are additional supports/resources needed?

_____

_____

What is intervention outcome? Was there a response to intervention?   Y / N

_____

_____

Have there been classroom observations for fidelity?   Y / N
Have there been classroom observations for documentation of curriculum, learner, and
environmental variables?   Y / N

Week_____Tier _____
Are the interventions being implemented as designed?   Y / N
If not, why not?_____

_____

Are additional supports/resources needed?

_____

_____

What is intervention outcome? Was there a response to intervention?   Y / N

_____

_____

Have there been classroom observations for fidelity?   Y / N
Have there been classroom observations for documentation of curriculum, learner, and
environmental variables?   Y / N

Week_____Tier _____
Are the interventions being implemented as designed?   Y / N
If not, why not?_____

_____

Are additional supports/resources needed?

_____

_____

What is intervention outcome? Was there a response to intervention?   Y / N

_____

_____

Have there been classroom observations for fidelity?   Y / N
Have there been classroom observations for documentation of curriculum, learner, and
environmental variables?   Y / N

RtI Documentation of Tier 1 Instructional Interventions: Basic Reading

Student: _____   Teacher(s): _____

Student Date of Birth: _____   Grade: _____   Date of Review: _____   Case Facilitator: _____

Instruction and Curriculum			Tier 1 Core Instruction Supports		
Targeted Area of Instruction	Description of Participation in Core Curriculum (amount of time, mode of instruction, lesson plan objectives)	Has Student Been Provided Appropriate Core Curriculum?	Strategies (interventions)	Consistency of Implementation	Fidelity Check
Phonemic awareness		Yes No		Attendance Work samples Formative assessment	Fidelity check Classroom observations Lesson plan review
Phonics		Yes No		Attendance Work samples Formative assessment	Fidelity check Classroom observations Lesson plan review
Fluency		Yes No		Attendance Work samples Formative assessment	Fidelity check Classroom observations Lesson plan review
Vocabulary		Yes No		Attendance Work samples Formative assessment	Fidelity check Classroom observations Lesson plan review
Comprehension		Yes No		Attendance Work samples Formative assessment	Fidelity check Classroom observations Lesson plan review

We assure that the above-noted intervention or interventions were conducted as disclosed.

_____   _____   _____
Principal/RtI Team Chair   Classroom Teacher/Service Provider   Case Facilitator

RtI Documentation of Tier 1 Instructional Interventions: Reading Literacy

Student: _____

Student Date of Birth: _____   Grade: _____   Date of Review: _____   Teacher(s): _____   Case Facilitator: _____

Instruction and Curriculum			Tier 1 Core Instruction Supports	
Targeted Area of Instruction	Description of Participation in Core Curriculum (amount of time, mode of instruction, lesson plan objectives)	Has Student Been Provided Appropriate Core Curriculum?	Strategies (interventions)	Consistency of Implementation	Fidelity Check
Fluency of text reading		Yes No		Attendance Work samples Formative assessment	Fidelity check Classroom observations Lesson plan review
Vocabulary (as defined as the breadth and depth of knowledge about the meaning of words)		Yes No		Attendance Work samples Formative assessment	Fidelity check Classroom observations Lesson plan review
Comprehension		Yes No		Attendance Work samples Formative assessment	Fidelity check Classroom observations Lesson plan review
Background knowledge related to content of text		Yes No		Attendance Work samples Formative assessment	Fidelity check Classroom observations Lesson plan review
Higher-level reasoning skills		Yes No		Attendance Work samples Formative assessment	Fidelity check Classroom observations Lesson plan review
Motivation and engagement for understanding and learning from text		Yes No		Attendance Work samples Formative assessment	Fidelity check Classroom observations Lesson plan review

We assure that the above-noted intervention or interventions were conducted as disclosed.

_____   _____   _____
Principal/RtI Team Chair   Classroom Teacher/Service Provider   Case Facilitator

RtI Documentation of Tier 1 Instructional Interventions: Written Language

Student: _____ Teacher(s): _____

Student Date of Birth: _____ Grade: _____ Date of Review: _____ Case Facilitator: _____

Instruction and Curriculum			Tier 1 Core Instruction Supports		
Targeted Area of Instruction	Description of Participation in Core Curriculum (amount of time, mode of instruction, lesson plan objectives)	Has Student Been Provided Appropriate Core Curriculum?	Strategies (interventions)	Consistency of Implementation	Fidelity Check
Writing content		Yes No		Attendance Work samples Formative assessment	Fidelity check Classroom observations Lesson plan review
Mechanics of writing		Yes No		Attendance Work samples Formative assessment	Fidelity check Classroom observations Lesson plan review

We assure that the above-noted intervention or interventions were conducted as disclosed.

_____ _____ _____
Principal/RtI Team Chair   Classroom Teacher/Service Provider   Case Facilitator

RtI Documentation of Tier 1 Instructional Interventions: Math

Student: _____

Student Date of Birth: _____ Grade: _____ Date of Review: _____ Case Facilitator: _____

Teacher(s): _____

Targeted Area of Instruction	Tier 1 Core Instruction Supports			
	Instructional Strategies (interventions)		Consistency of Implementation	Fidelity Check
Math concepts and problem solving	Explicit instruction	Y N		
	Multiple examples	Y N		
	Think-aloud approach	Y N	Attendance	Fidelity check
	Visual representations to problem-solve	Y N	Work samples	Classroom observations
	Use of multiple heuristic strategies	Y N	Formative assessment	Lesson plan review
	Peer-assisted instruction	Y N		
Mechanics of writing	Explicit instruction	Y N		
	Multiple examples	Y N		
	Think-aloud approach	Y N	Attendance	Fidelity check
	Visual representations to problem-solve	Y N	Work samples	Classroom observations
	Use of multiple heuristic strategies	Y N	Formative assessment	Lesson plan review
	Peer-assisted instruction	Y N		

We assure that the above-noted intervention or interventions were conducted as disclosed.

_____ _____ _____
Principal/RtI Team Chair   Classroom Teacher/Service Provider   Case Facilitator

Notification of Tier 2 RtI Team Meeting

To: _____Date: _____

Purpose: RtI team meeting to discuss Tier 1 interventions and progress. Please be prepared to present documentation of curriculum, instruction, interventions, and any other data you have collected on the following child to the RtI team.

Student:_____Grade: _____

Please bring copies of the following, as applicable. Check off each item as it is filed:

_____ Documentation of Tier 1 Instruction and Interventions form
_____Attendance records
_____Health screening
_____Multiple intelligence Learning profile
_____Grades printout
_____Photocopies of all standardized and criterion-referenced tests/assessment data
_____ARI/AMI/title documentation
_____Lesson plans
_____Student work samples (e.g, journal, spelling tests, math computation)
_____Discipline record printout
_____Any other documentation that shows Tier 1 classroom interventions
_____Home Language Survey
_____Parent conference documentation

If you have any questions, please contact an RtI team member before your assigned time.

Thank you,

_____
RtI Team Chair

Documentation of Tier 2/Tier 3 RtI Team Meeting

Student:_____Teacher: _____

Case Facilitator:_____Date of Meeting: _____

Step 1: Problem Identification

- Tier 1 Instructional strategies used and student outcomes
- Core curriculum support documentation
- Academic engagement strategies documentation
- Student multiple intelligence profiles and learning inventories
- Student work samples
- Lesson plans/schedules
- Assessments (including but not limited to fluency probes, common assessments, and district benchmarks)
- Additional Tier 1 strategies used
- Any additional data (e.g., attendance and tardy records, parent contacts, conferences)

Step 2: Inventory of Student Strengths and Talents

Step 3: Health and Other Variables Affecting Learning

Documentation indicates:

Step 4: Selection of Targeted Areas of Intervention

List two targeted concerns:

1. _____

2. _____

Note: Add these concerns to the Targeted Area of Instruction section on the Documentation of Tier 2 or 3 Intervention and Assessment form.

Step 5: Baseline Data Review and Goal Setting

Content area: _____Instructional level: _____

Goals (expected weekly growth and number of intervention weeks):

Step 6: Design of Intervention Plan

Hypothesis statement: _____
_____

Strategic intervention(s) identified: _____

Where: _____

When: _____

Resources needed:

Interventionist assigned: _____

Data collector (progress monitoring): _____

Step 7: Method of Progress Monitoring

Data collector:_____

Where: _____

When: _____

Fidelity check (date):_____

Step 8: Parent Communication Plan

Parent contact: _____

Time: _____

Step 9: Intervention and Monitoring Review

Members in agreement?   ____Yes   ___ No

Follow-up meeting date:_____

Case manager consultation follow-up date:_____

Step 10: Signature record *(All members in attendance sign.)*

Name	Position
	Chairperson
	Teacher of Record
	Case Manager
	Timekeeper
	Data Manager
	Scribe
	Interventionist
	Team Member
	Team Member
	Parent

RtI Documentation: Tier 2/Tier 3 Intervention and Assessment

Interventionist: _____ Student: _____ Grade: _____ Tier: _____

Instructional Skill(s)/Level	Date	Day of Week	No. of Minutes	Progress-Monitoring Data
		M T W Th F		CBM probe level _____ WCPM _____ DCPM _____ BCPM
		M T W Th F		CBM probe level _____ WCPM _____ DCPM _____ BCPM
		M T W Th F		CBM probe level _____ WCPM _____ DCPM _____ BCPM
		M T W Th F		CBM probe level _____ WCPM _____ DCPM _____ BCPM
		M T W Th F		CBM probe level _____ WCPM _____ DCPM _____ BCPM
		M T W Th F		CBM probe level _____ WCPM _____ DCPM _____ BCPM
		M T W Th F		CBM probe level _____ WCPM _____ DCPM _____ BCPM
		M T W Th F		CBM probe level _____ WCPM _____ DCPM _____ BCPM
		M T W Th F		CBM probe level _____ WCPM _____ DCPM _____ BCPM
		M T W Th F		CBM probe level _____ WCPM _____ DCPM _____ BCPM
		M T W Th F		CBM probe level _____ WCPM _____ DCPM _____ BCPM
		M T W Th F		CBM probe level _____ WCPM _____ DCPM _____ BCPM

Abbreviations: WCPM, words correct per minute; DCPM, digits correct per minute; BCPM, behaviors correct per minute.

RTI Fidelity Checklist: Tier 1 Curriculum and Instruction Strategies

Student: _____

Grade: _____

Date and Time: _____

Teacher: _____

Class Size: _____

Observer: _____

Grouping: _____ Whole-Class Instruction _____ Small Group _____ Paired _____ Individual (1:1)

Description of Lesson Objective:

Specific to Core Instruction Delivery:

Yes	Sometimes	No	Not Observed	Observation Descriptor	Notes
				Lesson plan objective is clearly communicated to students.	
				Lesson plan objectives are evident in student work samples.	
				Teacher delivers instruction consistent with lesson plan objectives.	
				Delivery of instruction allows time for practice of objective.	
				Teacher has necessary resources to differentiate content, process, and product.	
				Teacher-student interactions are positive, reinforcing strong teacher-student relationships.	
				Teacher provides continuous constructive feedback to students.	
				Measured academic engagement time of class is high.	

Specific to Differentiation of Content for Struggling Student(s):   *(Check all that are observed.)*

Cooperative Learning	Learning Environment	Student Products	Differentiation	Suggestions
___ Small group ___ Cooperative learning roles ___ Variety of criteria for grouping Other: ___ ___	___ Classroom management ___ Classroom organization ___ Classroom centers ___ Behavior rules posted ___ Student objectives posted ___ Reinforcing effort Other: ___ ___ ___	___ Physical representations (models, books, etc.) ___ Musical representations ___ Poetry ___ Dramatic responses (play, role-playing, reenactment) Other: ___ ___	___ Student work samples ___ Presentation of material ___ Use of manipulatives ___ Classroom organization ___ Use of visual representations	

Multiple Intelligences	Questioning Strategies	Research-Based Strategies	Notes
___ Print—printed or written word ___ Aural—listening ___ Interactive verbalization ___ Visual—seeing visual descriptions such as pictures and graphs ___ Haptic—sense of touch or grasp ___ Kinesthetic—whole-body movement ___ Olfactory—smell and taste	___ Linguistic intelligence ("word smart") ___ Logical-mathematical intelligence ("number/reasoning smart") ___ Spatial intelligence ("picture smart") ___ Bodily-kinesthetic intelligence ("body smart") ___ Musical intelligence ("music smart") ___ Interpersonal intelligence ("people smart") ___ Intrapersonal intelligence ("self smart") ___ Naturalist intelligence ("nature smart")	___ Implicit vs. explicit questions ___ Higher order vs. lower order ___ Analytical ___ Reflective ___ Summarizing ___ Wait time ___ Modeling ___ Anchor activities ___ 4-step problem-solving approach ___ Timed drills to increase fluency ___ Use of student response cards ___ Graphic organizers ___ Vocabulary instruction ___ Self-monitoring chart ___ Homework planner	

RtI Fidelity Checklist: Tier 2/Tier 3 Interventions

Student: _____ Interventionist: _____ Grade: _____

Date and Time: _____ Observer: _____

Grouping: _____ Small Group _____ Paired _____ Individual (1:1)

Description of Instructional Level Lesson Objective:

Specific to Delivery of Intervention:

Yes	No	Not Observed	Observation Descriptor	Notes
			Intervention skill-building objective is clearly communicated to students.	
			Intervention objectives are evident in student work samples.	
			Interventionist delivers instruction consistent with program design.	
			Intervention level matches student instructional level (measured at baseline).	
			Repeated practice of objectives is aligned with measured skill deficits.	
			Interventionist has necessary resources to deliver intervention as designed.	
			Interventionist provides continuous constructive feedback to students.	
			Documented intervention time is consistent with RtI plan.	

RtI Team End-of-Year Review: Tier Summary Data

Campus: _____ Review Date: _____ Chair: _____

	Tier 1	Tier 2	Tier 3	Special Education Referrals		Movement between Tiers			
				Number Referred	Number Qualified	1 → 2	2 → 3	3 → 2	2 → 1
Kindergarten									
Reading									
Math									
Behavior									
Grade 1									
Reading									
Math									
Behavior									
Grade 2									
Reading									
Math									
Behavior									
Grade 3									
Reading									
Math									
Behavior									
Grade 4									
Reading									
Math									
Behavior									
Grade 5									
Reading									
Math									
Behavior									
Campus Totals	Tier 1	Tier 2	Tier 3	Number Referred	Number Qualified	1 → 2	2 → 3	3 → 2	2 → 1
Reading									
Math									
Behavior									

Bibliography

American Recovery and Reinvestment Act of 2009 (ARRA). http://frwebgate
.access.gpo.gov/cgi-bin/getdoc.cgi?dbname=111_cong_bills&docid=f:h1enr
.pdf.

Americans with Disabilities Act of 1990 (ADA). www.ada.gov/pubs/ada.htm.

Batsche, G., J. Elliot, J. L. Graden, J. Grimes, J. F. Kovaleski, D. Prasse, D. J. Reschly,
J. Schrag, and W. D. Tilly III. 2005. *Response to intervention: Policy considerations
and implementation.* Alexandria, VA: National Association of State Directors of
Special Education.

Bradley, R., L. Danielson, and D. P. Hallahan, eds. 2002. *Identification of learning disabilities: Research to practice.* Mahwah, NJ: Lawrence Erlbaum Associates.

Burrus, B. B., and I. F. Wallace. 2008. Evaluation: Conducting a sound process evaluation. Presentation at OAPP National Care and Prevention Conference, De-
cember 9 and 11.

Education Commission of the States. N.d. *NCLB highly qualified teacher and para-
professional database.* www.ecs.org/ecsmain.asp?page=/html/educationissues
/teachingquality/housse/houssedb_intro.asp.

Fiarman, S. E. 2007. Planning to assess progress: Mason Elementary School refines
an instructional strategy. In K. P. Boudett and J. L. Steele, eds., *Data Wise in action: Stories of schools using data to improve teaching and learning,* 125–148. Cam-
bridge, MA: Harvard Education Press.

Flowers, N., S. B. Mertens, and P. F. Mullhall. 1999. The impact of teaming: Five
research-based outcomes. *Middle School Journal* 31 (2): 1–6.

Fuchs, L., D. Fuchs, J. Hintze, and E. Lembke. 2006. Progress monitoring in the
context of Responsiveness-to-Intervention. Paper presented at the National
Center on Student Progress Monitoring Summer Institute, Kansas City, MO.

Furrer, C., and E. Skinner. 2003. Sense of relatedness as a factor in children's academic engagement and performance. *Journal of Educational Psychology* 95 (1):
148–162.

Gresham, F. M., D. L. MacMillan, M. E. Beebe-Frankenberger, and K. M. Bocian.
2000. Treatment integrity in learning disabilities intervention research: Do we
really know how treatments are implemented? *Learning Disabilities Research and
Practice* 15 (4): 198–205.

Hagermoser Sanetti, L., and T. R. Kratochwill. 2005. Treatment integrity assessment within a problem-solving model. In R. Brown-Chidsey, ed., *Problem-solving based assessment for educational intervention*, 304–325. New York: Guilford Press.

Halverson, R., R. B. Prichett, and J. G. Watson. 2007. *Formative feedback systems and the new instructional leadership*. Madison: Wisconsin Center for Education Research, University of Wisconsin.

Halverson, R., and C. N. Thomas. 2008. Student services practices as a model for data-driven instructional leadership. In M. M. Mangin and S. R. Stoelinga, eds., *Effective teacher leadership: Using research to inform and reform*, 163–182. New York: Teachers College Press.

Hasbrouck, J., and G. A. Tindal. 2006. Oral reading fluency norms: A valuable assessment tool for reading teachers. *Reading Teacher* 59 (7): 636–644.

Hill, D., J. Lewis, and J. Pearson. 2008. *Metro Nashville Public Schools student assessment staff development model*. Nashville, TN: Vanderbilt University, Peabody College.

Individuals with Disabilities Education Improvement Act (IDEA). 1997. PL 105-17. www2 ed.gov/policy/speced/leg/idea/idea.pdf.

Martin, Jose L. 2010. Child-Find in the RtI era. Do we really understand it? Paper presented at Border Conference, El Paso, TX.

McKenna, M. C., and K. A. Dougherty Stahl. 2009. *Assessment for reading instruction.* 2nd ed. New York: Guilford Press.

Mieles, T., and E. Foley. 2005. *From data to decisions: Lessons from school districts using data warehousing.* Providence, RI: Annenberg Institute for School Reform at Brown University. www.annenberginstitute.org/pdf/DataWarehousing.pdf.

NASDSE. 2005. *Response to Intervention: Policy considerations and implementation.* Alexandria, VA: National Association of State Directors of Special Education.

National Center on Response to Intervention. 2010. *Essential components of RTI— a closer look at Response to Intervention.* Washington, DC. www.rti4success.org /pdf/rtiessentialcomponents_042710.pdf.

No Child Left Behind Act of 2001 (NCLB). PL 107-110. www.ed.gov/policy /elsec/leg/esea02/107-110.pdf.

Office for Civil Rights. 2011. Protecting students with disabilities: Frequently asked questions about Section 504 and the education of children with disabilities. www2.ed.gov/about/offices/list/ocr/504faq.html.

Ogonosky, A. 2009. *Response to Intervention in Secondary Schools: How to Implement RtI in Middle and High Schools.* Austin, TX: Park Place Publications.

———. 2010. *RtI—FAQs: Straightforward Answers to the Most Common Questions from School Administrators, Teachers, and Parents.* Austin, TX: Park Place Publications.

Ogonosky, A., and K. Mintsioulis. 2010. *RtI—Three Tiers of Behavior: Strategies and Programs That Work!* Austin, TX: Park Place Publications.

Tomlinson, C. A., and J. McTighe. 2006. *Integrating differentiated instruction & Un-*

derstanding by design: Connecting content and kids. Alexandria, VA: Association for Supervision and Curriculum Development.

US Department of Education. 2004. New No Child Left Behind flexibility: Highly qualified teachers. Fact sheet. www2.ed.gov/nclb/methods/teachers /hqtflexibility.pdf.

Witt, J. C., A. M. VanDerHeyden, and D. Gilbertson. 2004. Instruction and classroom management: Prevention and intervention research. In R. B. Rutherford, M. M. Quinn, and S. R. Mathur, eds., *Handbook of research in emotional and behavioral disorders,* 426–445. New York: Guilford Press.

Andrea Ogonosky received her PhD in school psychology from Pennsylvania State University. She has practiced as a school psychologist in Pennsylvania and Texas and is the author of *The Response to Intervention Handbook: Moving from Theory to Practice; Response to Intervention in Secondary Schools: How to Implement RtI in Middle and High Schools; RtI—Three Tiers of Behavior: Strategies and Programs That Work!* (coauthored with Karen Mintsioulis); and *RtI—FAQs: Straightforward Answers to Questions from School Administrators, Teachers, and Parents.* She has written several articles on curriculum-based measurement, Response to Intervention, and working with struggling learners in the general education classroom. Andrea has been employed as the coordinator of psychological and diagnostic services in the Humble Independent School District and served as an adjunct professor at University of Houston–Clear Lake. Currently Andrea is a national speaker on RtI and an educational consultant providing school districts with support in developing and implementing RtI. She also completes academic and behavioral assessments, supervises school psychologists, and provides staff development in the areas of curriculum-based measurement, RtI, ADHD, learning disability assessment, emotional disturbance, autism, and behavior management. Andrea is a past president of the Texas Association of School Psychologists. She resides in Houston, Texas, and can be contacted at aogonosky@msn.com or www.ogonoskylearning.com.

To order other products from Park Place Publications and its subsidiaries, visit www.ed311.com.